Illinois Central College
Learning Resource Center

THE ART OF LOVE

THE LOVES

THE ART OF BEAUTY

THE REMEDIES FOR LOVE

and

 A MIDLAND ORIGINAL

OVID

OVIDIUS NASO, Publius

THE ART OF LOVE

WITHDRAWN

translated by ROLFE HUMPHRIES

INDIANA UNIVERSITY PRESS • BLOOMINGTON

Sixth printing, 1963

INTRODUCTION

T HESE poems, the product of Ovid's late youth and jaunty middle age (he was born in 43 B.C., and the latest references in the poem allude to events of 2 or 1 B.C.) are, by and large, rather frivolous stuff. Ovid himself was a little uneasy over their quality, if we can judge by the occasional expostulations he puts in the mouth of this or that Muse, urging him to loftier and more serious tasks, and by the way he digresses from his theme for the sheer sake of storytelling, in the manner he later developed, with greater maturity of grace and command, in the narrative of the *Metamorphoses*. Seldom do we get so clear a view of the stages in a writer's progress.

Were these books newly published today, our more advanced librarians, with perhaps some misgivings as to their erotic quality, might set them out on the display shelves along with other works in the Self-Help, the "How to," the "Do it yourself" category. This Ovid would approve, and also be amused by, well knowing that his precepts were set forth with considerably more tongue-in-cheek reservations than those of, say, Dr. Peale or Mr. Carnegie. He would object, with both embarrassment and distaste, to being transferred to those shelves where stand the social historians, the recorders of folkways, the archivists of civilizations and cultures.

Yet how brightly and clearly, with evocative skill far beyond that

5

of the most dutiful and self-conscious researcher, he portrays the social life of ancient Rome! The society life of modern Rome would be more like it, for Ovid could not possibly have taken himself, nor be taken, for an Ancient. Romantic to the core, he lacked one quality we are inclined to impute to romantics, the sense of loneliness and frustration, the spirit of protest against the time. Ovid dearly loved his time, and perhaps that is why we can see it so illumined, the play of the fountains, the hum and stir of the streets, the crowds in the fashionable walks, the light of parties at evening, the theaters, the races, the shops, the comings and goings of the smart set, the chatter in boudoirs, the doors barred, or the window left adroitly open to the solicitous lover. For anything like this, we would have to go back, beyond Congreve, beyond *The Rape of the Lock,* all the way to Geoffrey Chaucer.

Every age probably regards itself as unique in its sexual sophistication; a thesis devoted to a comparative study, in this respect, of the Romans and ourselves would require more space than this introduction can afford. If we take Ovid as a typical spokesman (Catullus and Martial do not sound like him at all), we should have to conclude that the keynote was elegance. This imposes, on the translator of the mid-twentieth century, considerable burden, for the language of our time, when we dwell on such matters, is very unlike Ovid's, our laymen, at times, employing the idiom of clerks Freud and Jung, a case-history sort of terminology, and, at other times, even in U circles, affecting a very non-U vernacular indeed. Ovid is much more even than we can be, his tone much more all of a piece, his conventions more consistent; one likes to suppose that, were he among us today, he would be responsive and adaptable enough to draw on whatever resource was offered, picking up whatever seemed lively, not only from the bright salon, but from stage and screen, not only from the purlieus of Bohemia, but from the slickness and sleekness of the advertising pages. So that, while violence may here have been done his letter, we have not, we hope, offended against his spirit.

6

His experiences we can readily recognize and believe, even when he is patently lying about them for artistic purposes, to round out a book, to complete a cycle. *Mutatis mutandis*, we have been through all enacted on this same divan or bed, we have resorted to the same gambits, we have been gullible enough to employ the same specifics, we have been equally rejoiced or disillusioned. He can be, by turns, boastful, indignant, abject, rueful, sly, lighthearted—in the latter respect, only, a bit alien to ourselves. So plausible is he, so apparently complete, that we hardly miss his failure to instruct us on two points—How to Seduce a Virgin, and How to Offer a Proposal of Marriage.

He is not, in these books, a very careful writer, though, line by line, he is an extremely polished one. He repeats himself a good deal, is inconsistent (this he knows), gets drawn away from his subject, uses too many illustrations, and, in one instance at least (*The Art of Love*, Book I, lines 177-216), gives way to such ghastly political sycophancy in praise of the young Caesar against the Parthians* that I was tempted to leave out the whole passage. But it is not the translator's responsibility, under these circumstances, to edit or anthologize his subject, so I kept going and was presently struck by a not so Roman thought. Could it have been possible that this was a most brazen example of Ovidian impudence, that he was writing this deliberately, as who should say, "Well, this is the kind of stuff they want, so, by God, they can have it!" A comforting thought, and just as apt as not to be wrong.

In translating these poems, I have, in the main, approximated Ovid's original meter, the elegiac distich, using, as he did, internal rhyming occasionally in the shorter lines. One advantage of this system is that we come out, line for line, and couplet for couplet,

---

* The young Caesar was Augustus' grandson, heading an expedition against Phraates, King of the Parthians. In this campaign he died of a wound, which seems no more than he deserved, by way of poetic justice, for having inspired such writing and making Ovid look bad as both poet and prophet.

pretty close to the original length; Ovid had a tendency, as Professor L. P. Wilkinson points out, to sow with the sack and not the hand, so where he has supported an argument with illustrations that would involve the reader in meaningless allusion and an excess of proper names, I have sometimes cut a bit. *Per contra*, once in a while I have worked into his text explanations that might otherwise have to be incorporated in footnotes or glossary. I say *approximated* his meter, because English does not run as readily into spondees as Latin does, and the reader who wants to hear the tone of the original as obbligato should be reminded that our disposition toward the trochee does produce a line somewhat flipper than Latin, even when the matter is not itself unduly solemn. I say *in the main*, because in some of the shorter poems from *The Loves*, I have used the Shakespearean sonnet form. This for two reasons: to add an element of variety, and also because, it seems to me, there is a relationship between sonnet and elegy, not only in the proportions, but also in the spirit. In these sonnets, of course, both the brevity of the line and the exigencies of rhyme have taken me farther away from the letter of Ovid.

To sum up: *The Loves* and *The Art of Love*, while not the fruit of Ovid's maturest opulence, are a good deal closer to the *Metamorphoses* than is *Love's Labour's Lost*, say, to *The Tempest*. We can enter into these poems in the spirit of King Evander's invitation to Aeneas, "Dare, O my guest, to think of wealth as nothing," remembering that they gave delight to spirits as unkindred as Dafydd ap Gwilym and Dante, Marlowe and Milton, Petrarch and Pope Pius II. The fifth husband of the Wife of Bath had *The Art of Love* in his library, and it might be well to leave the final word of introduction to the author of *The Canterbury Tales*, who gives us

> "Venus clerk, Ovyde,
> That hath y-sowen wonder-wyde
> The grete god of loves name."

New York City
January, 1957

ROLFE HUMPHRIES

CONTENTS

THE LINE NUMBERS AT THE TOP OF EACH TEXT PAGE
ARE THOSE OF THE LATIN TEXT IN THE LOEB EDITION

THE LOVES

THE EPIGRAPH

Five books once we were, but now, in the second edition,
   Ovid, our author, saw fit to cut us down quite a bit.
So there are three of us now, and if we give you no pleasure,
   Still, your pains may be less with two of us taken away.

BOOK

I

I

Arms and violent wars, with meter suited to matter,
    Arms and violent wars, all in hexameters,
I was preparing to sound, when I heard a snicker from Cupid;
    What had the rascal done, but taken one foot away?
"Why, you bad boy!" I said, "who gave you this jurisdiction?
    We are the Muses' own, not your contemptible throng.
What if Venus should snatch the arms of fair-haired Minerva,
    What if Minerva should fan torches of love into flame?
Who would approve it if Ceres ruled on the ridges of woodland,
    Tilling the fields that law gave to Diana for hers?
How would Apollo learn to brandish a sharp-pointed spear-shaft?
    Wouldn't Mars look like a fool strumming the Orphean lyre?
You have an empire, my boy, thrones and dominions and powers,
    Is there no end to ambition? Why do you claim any more?
Or is everything yours, and Helicon only a province,
    Apollo a captive prince, hardly sure of his lyre?
My first line rose well, noble and lofty in measure,
    But the one you brought next surely corrupted the text.
What can I do in light verse? I have no boy I can sing of,
    No nice long-haired girl making a theme for my lays."

So I complained, and he drew out a shaft from his quiver,
    Taking his time to choose just the right arrow to use,
Bent the bow, moon-shaped, at his knee, and "Poet," he told me,
    "Take what I send; this barb surely will sting you to song!"
Never was truer word spoken; that boy shot straight with his arrow,
    I am on fire, and my heart owns the dominion of love,
So let my work arise in the manner called elegiac:
    Good riddance, iron wars; good riddance, hexameters!
Now let my golden-haired Muse adorn herself with the myrtle,
    Dark-green, loving the ground, loved by the goddess of love.

II

What kind of business is this? The bed is hard, and the covers
    Will not stay in their place; I thrash, and I toss, and I turn
All the long night through, till my bones are utterly weary.
    What's the matter with me? am I a victim of love?
I didn't think so, but—yes, that must be the cause of the trouble,
    Heartache, fever of love feeding the fire in my breast.
Do we give in, or exasperate fire by a struggle against it?
    Better give in, and so lighten the weight of the load.
I have seen fire blaze up when torches are swung in a circle,
    Seen them die down again, soon as you let them alone.
Oxen who fight the yoke of the plough take more of a beating,
    Horses that learn to submit hurt less from bridle and bit.
Love is a driver, bitter and fierce if you fight and resist him,
    Easy-going enough once you acknowledge his power.
Look! I confess! I am prey, I am plunder and spoil for you, Cupid;
    Beaten, I reach out my hands, taking the bonds of your law.
Little your praise if you capture a raw recruit, all defenseless—
    There is no need for a war; pardon and peace is my prayer.
Bind the temples with myrtle, harness the doves of your mother,
    Ride in a chariot of Mars, taking the cheers of the crowd!
Young men and girls will follow, prisoners in the procession,

Far as the eye can reach, adding to pomp and parade,
And I will come dragging along, humbled, my wound fresh upon me,
    Bearing my captive chain with what endurance I can.
Conscience, her hands bound behind her, will march in the ranks of
    the vanquished;
    Modesty, too, will be there—all the opponents of love.
All will bow down before you, all will be chanting Hosannas,
    All with one great voice render you homage and praise.
And your camp-followers all, Folly, Illusion, and Madness,
    All that undisciplined crew dance their attendance on you.
Such are the legions you use in subduing both men and immortals,
    Take them away and you stand naked, no weapon at hand.
Oh, and your mother will watch and cheer the triumphal procession,
    Showering roses down for the parade of her son.
Golden, on golden wheels, ride to your golden glory,
    Jewels decking your wings, jewels decking your hair.
More than a few will be burnt by the golden flame, if I know you,
    More than a few be found hurt with a deadly wound.
Even against your will, the fiery flight of the arrows
    Still would flash and the fire wither everything near.
So rode Bacchus in pride over the Indian victims,
    Drawn by his tigers; you are equally feared with your doves.
So, since I must be part of the spectacle, spare me,
    Spend on me no more all the full force of your power.
Be a good boy for once, and learn a lesson from Caesar
    Whose victorious hand raises the victim he felled.

III

Fair play, I pray; let her who preys on me
Love me, or give me reason for her praise.
Ah, I have asked too much, I plainly see.
Let her be loved, let Venus guide my ways.
Take me, who for long years would be your slave;

Take me, who know devotion, deep and pure:
I have no pride of ancestors; I have
No name to recommend me, I am sure.

My father was a tradesman, and the ploughs
That till my land are far from numberless.
My parents owned a cottage, not a house,
And still watch money closely, I confess.
But at my side Apollo and the Nine
Attend, and Bacchus, finder of the vine.

And Love is on my side, who gives to you
Myself as gift, a man of modest ways,
Decent behavior, and a faith as true
As you are apt to find in all your days.
And I am not promiscuous, I swear—
Whatever skein of life the Sisters give
I would devote to your eternal care,
And when I die, be lucky if you grieve.

Give me yourself as matter for my song,
The songs will issue worthy of their cause.
Europa, Io, Leda live as long
As men keep reading poets with applause.
So may our legend last while verse endures
And all that time my name be linked with yours.

IV

So, that husband of yours is going to be at the party—
    Well, I hope he chokes; let him drop dead, who cares?
How am I going to act?—just stare at the girl I'm in love with,
    Be just one more guest, let some one else feel your breast,
Let some one else put his arms around you whenever he wants to,

Sit at your side, rub knees, lean on your shoulder a bit?
I can believe what they say of the brawls of the Lapiths and Centaurs
    Over the fair-haired girl, after the wine went round.
I do not live in the woods, and my members are not like a horse's,
    Still I'll be having a time keeping my hands to myself.
Learn what you have to do, and please pay careful attention:
    Get there before he does—not that that does any good.
Anyway, get there before him, and when he reclines, you beside him,
    Modestly on the couch, give my foot just a touch,
Watch me for every nod, for every facial expression,
    Catch my signs and return them, never saying a word.
I can talk with my eyebrows and spell out words with my fingers,
    I can make you a sign, dipping my finger in wine.
When you think of the tumbles we've had in the hay together,
    Touch your cheek with your hand; then I will understand.
If you're a little bit cross with the way I may be behaving,
    Let your finger-tip rest light on the lobe of an ear.
If, on the other hand, what I am saying should please you,
    Darling, keep turning your ring; symbol enough that will be.
Fold your hands on the table, as people do when they're praying—
    That means you wish him bad luck, yes, and a lot of it, too.
When he mixes your wine, let him drink it himself; so inform him:
    Quietly speak to the boy, ask for the kind you enjoy.
When you pass him the cup, let me have a sip as it goes by;
    Where you drank I will touch that part first with my lips.
Don't accept any food from a dish that he has first tasted;
    Keep his arms from your neck; don't lay your head on his chest;
Don't let his fingers grope in the neck of your dress or your bosom;
    More than everything else, don't let him kiss you at all.
Don't you kiss him, either; you do, and you'll have me announcing
    "Hands off there! She's mine"—and then I'll reach out for my
        claim.
All these things I can watch, but the acts that the robe is disguising
    Rouse all my blind fears; what I can't see is the worst.

Don't press knee to knee, nor let your thigh rub against him;
    Don't let your delicate toe touch those clodhoppers of his.
I am afraid of much, because I have made my own passes,
    So my torment is worse, knowing the way it goes.
Often—haven't we, dear?—we have had to hurry our pleasure
    Rushing the sweet caress under the folds of the dress.
This you will not do; but, lest you be thought to have done it,
    Let the cloak slip down, leaving the shoulders bare.
Let him drink all he wants; keep urging him, only don't kiss him.
    Keep on filling his glass, secretly, if you can.
Once he passes out cold, perhaps we can figure out something—
    Time and circumstance maybe will give us a chance.
When you rise to go home, and the rest of the company rises,
    Try as hard as you can to move in the thick of the throng.
You will find me there in the crowd, or else, be sure, I will find you,
    If you can reach me there, lay your hand on my arm.
Ah, but what good does this do? It is good for a few hours only.
    Separation draws near, separation, and night.
At night he will lock you in, and I, all gloomy and tearful,
    Follow as far as I dare, up to the cruel door.
Then he'll get kisses from you, and get, I guess, more than kisses.
    What I cheat for, he owns; what can you do but give in?
But—this much you can do—give in as if you disliked it,
    Give in as if you were forced; don't say a word; be cold.
Venus hearing my prayer, there won't be much fun in it for him;
    And, if worst comes to worst, no fun at all for you.
Still, whatever occurs in the night, convince me, next morning
    What I would like to believe—tell me you slept alone.

V

    Hot noon, and I was lying on my bed,
    The window halfway open, and the light
    The way it is in woods, when sun has fled

After the day, before the coming night,
Or before day, after the night has gone,
For modest girls a reassuring shade,
Just the right sort of light, with curtains drawn,
Wherein to lay inviting ambuscade.

And there Corinna entered, with her gown
Loosened a little, and on either side
Of her white neck the dark hair hanging down.
Semiramis could not have been, as bride,
Any more lovely, nor could Lais move
The hearts of men more easily to love.

Sheer though it was, I pulled the dress away;
Pro forma, she resisted, more or less.
It offered little cover, I must say,
And why put up a fight to save a dress?
So soon she stood there naked, and I saw,
Not only saw, but felt, perfection there,
Hands moving over beauty without flaw,
The breasts, the thighs, the triangle of hair.

No need for catalogue, to itemize
All those delights, nor could I truly say
That I confined my pleasure to my eyes.
Naked, I took her, naked, till we lay
Worn out, done in. Grant me, O gods, the boon
Of many such another sultry noon!

VI

Doorkeeper—unworthy fate!—bound to the links of hard iron,
    Let the hinge turn, I pray; open the difficult door.
I am not asking much; half ajar is sufficient—
    If I stand sidewise and squeeze, that's all the room that I need.

Loving has made me thin, and taught me how to walk softly
    Past the guards of the night; love keeps my footsteps aright.
Once I was fearful of night, its darkness, shadows, and phantoms,
    Wondered how men would go where they might meet with a
      ghost.
Cupid and Venus laughed in my ear, both whispering "Courage!"
    Love came without delay; now I can go my way,
Fearing no spectre by night, no muggers stalking the darkness,
    Only one thing I fear, you and the bolt of my doom.
Look! and that you may see, swing the grim barrier open;
    See how the hinge has been stained, wet with the oil of my tears.
Wasn't it I, when you once stood stripped and ready for flogging,
    Trembling, wasn't it I who spoke to your lady for you?
Yes, and a lot of good my graciousness seems to have done me:
    The hours of the night go by; take the bar from the door.
Take the bar from the door, and may you be lightened forever
    Of the long chain, nor drink water with every slave.
Doorkeeper, iron heart, I am pleading with you: will you listen?
    No, the door stands stiff, braced with its bar of oak.
Towns under siege need bolts, need bars by way of protection;
    We are living in peace; what do you fear from arms?
What will you do to a foe, when you act this way with a lover?
    The hours of the night go by; take the bar from the door.
I do not come here, a host in arms, with battalions of soldiers,
    Save for implacable love, I am completely alone,
And even though I should wish, I cannot give him dismissal,
    That would tear from my side part of my actual self.
Love for an escort, and wine, a little, to give me some courage,
    I with my chaplet askew—what do you think I can do?
Who could fear such a threat? who would not cheerfully face it?
    The hours of the night go by; take the bar from the door.
Oh, but you're tough, or asleep, and the winds take the words of the
    lover.
    If you're asleep on the job, I hope it costs you, you slob.

But I remember at first when I wanted you not to notice,
    You were on guard, alert, until the midnight stars.
Possibly now, while you sleep, your girl is lying beside you:
    So much the better for you; so much the worse for me.
I could accept the chains, given that other condition—
    The hours of the night go by; take the bar from the door.
What do I hear? A sound? The raucous harshness of hinges?
    No, it was only the wind, beating, like me, on the door.
Boreas, if you recall the girl whom you took with your north wind,
    Come here, batter and blast this unanswering door.
All the city is still, and, dripping with dewdrops of crystal,
    The hours of the night go by; take the bar from the door.
Otherwise I myself, better armed with fire and with iron,
    Not with the torch in my hand, lay my assault to the door.
Night and love and wine hardly persuade moderation:
    Night has no shame; love and wine have no conception of fear.
I have tried everything now, and neither threats nor entreaties
    Serve to move you at all; you are as hard as the door.
Unbecoming, that you should guard a pretty girl's bedroom;
    You should watch in a jail, guarding some desperate cell.
Now the frost-white wheels of the dawn are already in motion,
    Now the bird of the dawn rouses poor men to their toil.
Lie there on the step, torn from my sorrowing temples,
    Chaplet, lie on the step, through the short remnant of night.
Tell her, in mute reproach, when she sees you there in the morning
    What a bad time I spent, while the bar remained on the door.
Doorkeeper, fare you well; though I owe you a grudge, I acknowl-
    edge,
    Tough though you were, you were true, keeping the lover away.
And you fellow-slaves, cruel doorposts, lintel and threshold,
    Yielding me nothing at all, leaving, I give you farewell.

VII

Friend—if I have a friend—put the handcuffs upon me
    Till the madness has passed; my hands have deserved to be tied.
Mad I must have been, to lift a hand to my sweetheart;
    The poor girl is in tears, hurt by my crazy blows.
I would have lashed out, then, at the holy gods and their altars,
    Even the parents I love might have felt my violent hands.
Well! did not Ajax, too, lord of the sevenfold aegis,
    Run amuck through the flocks, striking them down in the fields?
Did not Orestes avenge the adulterous guilt of his mother,
    Daring to ask for arms even against the Fates?
So that gave me the right, I suppose, to pull all her hair out!
    Still, her dishevelled hair hardly injured her looks.
She was beautiful, so, as lovely as Atalanta
    Hunting Maenalian game, armed with the quiver and dart.
So must another have seemed, Ariadne, lonely on Naxos,
    Weeping for Theseus, false, borne on the wind from the south.
So must Cassandra have looked before the shrine of Minerva;
    One slight difference, though—fillets were binding her hair.
Who did not scream at me then, "Madman! barbarian! sadist!"?
    She said never a word; she was too frightened to speak.
Even her silence, though, proclaimed me guilty, reproved me;
    Tears accused me of crime, even though lips were dumb.
I could wish that my arms had sooner dropped from my shoulders;
    I'd have been better off lacking those parts of myself.
All to my own hurt, I spent my strength in my madness;
    Put the handcuffs upon me—that is the fate I deserve.
Would I escape had I struck the lowest, the basest, of Romans?
    How did I ever acquire greater domain over her?
Diomed started it all, with his sacrilegious example,
    Striking a goddess and I followed his evil way.
He was less guilty than I, who kept my blows for a loved one.
    Diomed, anyway, thought he was striking a foe.

24

Go now, conquering hero, ride in majesty onward,
    Twine with laurel the brow, pay your homage to Jove,
Let the crowd follow your car, and cheer, exultant in triumph,
    "Hail, all-glorious prince, victor over a girl!"
Let her trudge on ahead, her hair dishevelled, a captive,
    White from head to foot save for the weals on her cheek.
Decenter, far, had I left bruises from too much kissing,
    Set, on her snowy neck, the sign of the bite of my teeth,
Or if I had to be swept away like the rush of a river,
    Raging full flood, the blind prey of my own angry mind,
Would it not have sufficed to scream at the poor little darling,
    Sparing the poor little dove threats more in order from Jove?
Couldn't I, like a beast, have ripped the gown from her shoulder
    All the way down to the waist, down to the girdle at least?
No! What I did was yank and tear the hair from her forehead,
    Clawing her freeborn cheeks with the rough slash of my nails.
There she stood in a daze, her features whiter than marble,
    Whiter than Parian stone hewn from the cliffs of the isle.
I saw her quiver in fear, I saw her limbs all a-tremble;
    So do the aspen-trees shake in the stir of the breeze,
So does the slender reed shudder when wind goes over,
    So does the ruffled wave answer the motion of air.
Then her tears, at long last, for she could no longer control them,
    Flooded, as water flows out of the melting of snow.
Then I first began to know myself for a scoundrel;
    Every tear she shed seemed like a drop of my blood.
Thrice I wanted to fall at her feet and beg her forgiveness;
    Thrice she pushed off my hands when they went out in appeal.
Vengeance will lessen remorse—claw at me, scratch at my features,
    Spare neither eyes nor hair; anger will make you strong.
Or, at the very least, to cancel my evil-doing,
    Or abolish its mark, straighten your hair with the comb.

VIII

Would you like to hear of a bawd? I know one, an old bag named
      Dipsas;
      Yes, and well-named, too, though Dipso or Tipsy would do.
Her name goes with the facts; never, in all her lifetime,
      Has she been sober at dawn, watching Aurora's steeds.
She knows magical arts, the incantations of Circe,
      She can make rivers turn, flowing back from the sea,
Knows about simples and herbs, the charms of the thread and the
      treadle,
      Knows how a mare in heat spreads a poison around.
Clouds at her will grow dark, thickening through the aether;
      Light, at her will, returns, and the blue heaven is bright.
I, believe it or not, have seen the stars raining crimson,
      Seen the face of the moon turn to the color of blood.
I suspect that at night she rides the sky on a broomstick,
      Turns to an owl or a crow, feathers all over her hide.
I suspect, and am told, that her eyes both have double pupils,
      And that lightning flies out of the blink of her eyes.
And she can call from the grave souls of the lost generations,
      Open the stones of the tomb with the long howl of her song.
This old hag has the gall to try to divorce us, from friendship!—
      That doesn't say that her tongue can't do us plenty of harm.
Luck let me hear what she said; I was back of the door, and in hid-
      ing,
      Listening hard as I could. These were the warnings she gave:
"Listen, honey; know something? Yesterday, that young fellow—
      He has plenty of money, and, dearie, he's stuck on you.
Well, why not? You're pretty, you have a wonderful figure,
      Only one thing in your way—you haven't nice enough clothes.
If you had only the luck you need to go with your beauty—
      If you were rich, I suppose, I wouldn't have to be poor.
I've read your horoscope. Mars was in opposition;

Mars has gone and now Venus is on your side.
Aren't you the lucky one, though?—here is a rich young fellow
 Wants you and willing to spend money to get what he wants;
Not bad-looking at all—you'd make a wonderful couple.
 If he's unwilling to buy, possibly he is for sale."
That made her blush, at least. But Dipsas went on with her chatter:
 "Blushing's a waste of time, only good when put on.
Keep your eyes cast down, your hands in your lap, that's modest,
 But get your ideas of a man out of the presents he brings.
Maybe, a long time ago, those Sabine girls were contented
 Sticking to one alone; that was a long time ago.
Mars may be somewhere testing the temper of lovers,
 But right here at home Venus is ruling in Rome.
Pretty girls ought to have fun, and purity—that's for the wallflowers;
 Only a hick's too coy not to go asking the boy.
Why do you wrinkle your forehead? That's just an act, and you
 know it:
 Smooth out the wrinkles, my dear; there is no place for them
 here.
What did Penelope mean when she gave the bow to the suitors,
 Testing their strength in the hall? which was most virile, that's
 all.
Time, in its gliding course, before we know it, is over;
 Time moves on chariot wheels drawn by galloping steeds.
Bronze grows bright with use, a nice dress needs to be modelled,
 Parts that you let alone moulder with long disuse.
Beauty, unless you give in, grows old if nobody takes it,
 And don't think one or two ever will satisfy you.
The more the better: the profit is greater, the gossip no meaner,
 Safety in numbers, my dear; not only safety, but gain.
What does that poet of yours ever give you except a new sonnet?
 Poems are a dime a dozen; you can have thousands to read.
Let him get dressed up in gold, like his lord and patron, Apollo;
 If he comes playing the lyre, see that the strings are of gold.

Homer a genius? Perhaps. But I think a millionaire's better.
    Giving, take it from me, is in itself quite an art.
Don't look down on a man if he's managed to purchase his freedom;
    Feet that have worn white chalk know how to make their own
        way.
Also, don't be fooled by collections of ancestors' portraits.
    Pick up your grandpa and go, lover without any dough!
Don't let them stay all night for free because they are handsome;
    Tell them to borrow or beg—maybe some girl would put out.
Take it easy at first; what was that bit I was reading?—
    In vain in the sight of the bird is the net of the fowler displayed.
After a while you can play them, and let them think that you love
        them;
    Once they think they are loved, get every present you can.
Hold out once in a while; tell them you have a bad headache,
    Say it's the time of the moon; that one they always believe.
After a while, let them in, before they get used to repulses;
    If they suffer too much from your frown, that's when desire will
        slow down.
Teach your door to be deaf to beggars, attentive to givers:
    Let the lover you take hear what the other one says.
Beat him to any reproach when you think he has cause for a griev-
        ance;
    Isn't the best defense always a good attack?
Don't overdo it too much, nor show too convincing a temper;
    Fury kept up too long drives them to somebody else.
Oh, and another good thing: learn to shed tears when you want to,
    And if the need should arise, don't be afraid to tell lies.
Train your servants and maids to hint, oh ever so subtly,
    What they've seen you admire, just the right present to buy.
Have them cadge for themselves little gifts; asking little from many,
    By and by, they will find, they have built up quite a pile.
Get your mother and sister and nurse to keep after your lover,
    Plunder that many seek comes more quickly to hand.

When you've no other excuse, you can always say it's your birthday,
    Show him the cake as proof rather than leave any doubt.
Don't let him take you for granted; throw out hints of a rival;
    Love too sure of its ground never endures very long.
Let him look at your bed and suspect that another man's been there,
    Let him find on your flesh some of the bruises of love,
Let him, above all else, see presents another has brought you—
    Maybe nobody has; then order some from the stores!
Much as he gives, don't let him hold out on you even a little;
    Coax him to make you a loan; this you need never return.
Flatter him while you work; let your tongue disguise your intention;
    Honey's the stuff to use for hiding the taste of the gall.
If you do as I say, and I've spent years in the business,
    If I'm not wasting my breath, just to hear myself talk,
You will be grateful to me, and thank me while I am living,
    After my death you will pray peace for my weary old bones."
She was still running on, when I was betrayed by my shadow,
    Making claws of my hands, ready to yank at her hair
(Not that she had very much), to give her a few good scratches
    Raking her wrinkled cheeks under her bleary old eyes.
May the gods give her old age no fire and many long winters,
    Finally may she be cursed with a continual thirst!

IX

Lovers are always at war, with Cupid watching the ramparts:
    Atticus, take it from me; lovers are always at war.
What's the right age for love?—the same as that for a soldier.
    How disgusting to all, old men at war, or in love!
What the captains demand, aggressiveness, ardor of spirit,
    That's what a pretty girl wants when a man's on the hunt.
Both keep watch all night, one at the tent of his captain
    On the hard ground, and one on the stone step of his girl.

The soldier's service is long, but send a girl on before him
    And the unfaltering lover plods the road without end.
Over the mountains he goes, through the rain-doubled rivers,
    Ploughing through snow piled deep, sailing the starless seas.
Who but a soldier or lover would bear the desolate seasons,
    Snow, sleet, gloom of night on his appointed rounds?
One is sent to observe the actions of enemy agents,
    The other, also, must spy; a rival is also a foe.
One lays siege to tall towns, the other his mistress's portals,
    One batters gateways down; one pounds away at a door.
Often success in war comes with the enemy's slumber—
    Rush in, then, and strike down all the unarmed of the town.
That was Diomed's way when he captured the horses of Rhesus
    And those Thracian steeds left their master behind.
Often success in love comes while a husband is sleeping;
    Lovers invading by dark use the appropriate tools;
Working their way through guards, eluding vigilant sentries,
    This is a task that tries soldier and lover alike.
Mars is a doubtful god, and Venus never too certain:
    Often the beaten rise; often invincibles fall.
Let it never be said that love is an indolent calling;
    Love is the test of a man ready for any proof.
While Achilles was moping over Briseis taken
    That was the time for Troy to shatter the Argive host.
From Andromache's arms Hector went rushing to battle—
    She was the one who set helmet and plume on his head.
Agamemnon stood spellbound at the sight of Cassandra,
    Daughter of Priam there, Maenad with streaming hair.
Mars caught in the toils forged by the cuckolded Vulcan:
    How the story went round all of Olympus knows well.
I was a lazy man, with a bent for bedroom and slippers,
    Doing what work I did half lying down in the shade.
Love for a beautiful girl took me out of the doldrums;
    When the order came, I sprang to arms in her camp.

So you see me alert and waging my wars in the night-time—
    If you want to forswear idleness, then fall in love!

X

Such as Helen was, when she left the banks of Eurotas,
    Leaving one lord for another, angel of war to them both;
Such as Leda was, whom Jupiter, crafty as lover,
    White in the radiant plumage, took in the guise of the swan;
Such as Amymone was, wandering over the parched lands,
    Bearing the urn on her head, walking majestic and tall;
Such were you, I thought, and was fearful of bull or of eagle
    Or whatever disguise Jove might assume for your eyes.
Now my fear is gone, my mind is cured of its error;
    All the charm you possessed troubles my sight no more.
Why? You well may ask. Because you are asking for money.
    If you please me no more, that is a good reason why.
While you were simple, I loved you, loved you, body and spirit,
    Now your beauty I find spoiled by the fault of your mind.
Love is a naked child: do you think he has pockets for money?
    Love is a naked child: do you think him for sale at a price?
Do you take them, mother and son, for mercenary campaigners,
    Harsh in the feats of war, serving for stipend or pay?
Tarts and call-girls wait, *prix fixe*, the demands of the market;
    They solicit, poor things, what the body can bring.
Yet even they curse out the percentage of pimp and of pander,
    Bargaining under duress. You do this on your own.
Take for example the beasts of the field; they are lacking in reason,
    Still, they are kinder than you—that is the final disgrace.
Heifers don't ask the bull for a gift, nor mares beg from stallions;
    Rams don't come to the ewe bringing a present or two.
Woman alone exults in the spoil she can take from a lover;
    Woman peddles her time and her place, and woman alone
Sells what both of them like, and what they both have been seeking,

Sells it, and sets the price high as the pleasure she gets.
Why should one cash in, when two of them get the enjoyment?
   Why should one sell it, and one have to pay for the fun?
Why do I have to lose, and you insist on a profit,
   When whatever we do brings equal pleasure to two?
Counsellors can't take fees if they know their clients are guilty;
   When their verdicts are bought, courts are considered corrupt.
Don't think going to bed for money is any less shameful:
   Beauty for sale at a price—what an abominable vice!
Thanks are, deservedly, due for offerings lavishly given;
   Love that is meanly hired rates no devotion at all.
Pay for it, and that's that—no more than a business transaction:
   No one's been gracious or sweet; no one's in anyone's debt.
Ah, my lovely ones, please—don't put a price on an evening!
   That kind of profit, I know, does you no good in the end.
Think of the case of Tarpeia—remember?—asking the Sabines
   What their left arms bore; wasn't she crushed by the shields?
Think of Eriphyle, seduced by desire of a necklace,
   Slain by Alcmaeon her son, treason and vengeance in one.
Still, it might not be so bad to ask for gifts from the wealthy;
   They have plenty to give; only let poets alone.
Where the vines hang full, reach out and plunder the clusters;
   Let Alcinous' field answer with generous yield.
But when a man is poor, all he can bring is devotion,
   That and a loyal heart as the award of his love.
I have a gift to confer, one gift, the power of my poems:
   Girls who deserve it will be not without honor from me.
Dresses rot into rags; the gold and the jewels will tarnish;
   Only the poet's song guarantees splendor for long.
Giving, that I don't mind: what I hate and despise is your asking;
   Ask me no more, and learn how I can give in return!

XI

You've been a good girl, Nippy, for a slave,
Giving good service in the stealthy night,
Adroit in brushing hair or setting wave,
Tipping me when I might not, when I might.
Often, when your Corinna was in doubt
Whether to come, your urging brought her here.
Take her this letter I have written out,
And let no other business interfere.

You have no flint or iron in your heart;
You are no simpler than you have to be.
Perhaps you too, wounded by Cupid's dart,
Could share campaign experience with me.
Tell her, in case she asks, that I am living
In hope of what, tonight, she may be giving.

The rest is in the letter, and the hour
Is flying. Take it to her! If you find
She does not say a word, you have the power,
Watching her countenance, to read her mind.
Urge her, when she has read, to write a lot—
I hate blank tablets like an empty stage—
Tell her to make the letters small, and not
Leave too much margin all along the page.

But no! That might tire out her pretty hand
Holding the pen. No need for that. She might
Put down two words, no more. I'd understand
If all the answer said was, "Come, tonight!"
I'd add a postscript: *Ovid's gratitude*
To Venus for this wax and maple wood.

XII

Weep my bad luck. The answer came back, "No!"
The answer said, "Impossible today."
Omens are something; Nippy stubbed her toe
This morning when she started on her way.
Next time, step higher, Nippy. As for you,
Disgusting tablets, gloomy wax and wood,
No wonder you acquired a blushing hue,
From minium, you claim; but I say blood.

Your wax, I think, was gathered from the flower
Of long-leaved hemlock, filched by Corsican bees,
Rank purgative, shipped in an evil hour.
As for the wood—you worse than useless trees!—
Lie where I fling you, on the dirty road;
Let the wheel break you, and the heavy load.

As for the lumberman who lopped your leaves
Converting you to use, the guilty wretch
Had better left you stand, to string up thieves
To give the neck of criminals a stretch,
To offer shadow for the nesting haunts
Of buzzards, owls, and other ugly birds.
Was it to you I trusted, like a dunce,
My fond endearments and my loving words?

Better such tablets hold the wordy writ
For some sour judge to read; better they lie
Among day-ledgers, suitable and fit
For tearful miser's avaricious eye.
Twin tablets, double dealers, and no good,
May old age fade your wax and rot your wood!

XIII

Over the ocean the bright one comes from her ancient Tithonus,
    Bringing with her the day, and the hoarfrost shines on her car.
"Dawdle a while, Aurora; wait while the starlings of Memnon
    Pay their annual rite, dark in the shadows of air.
Now is the time for me to lie in the arms of my darling;
    Now, if ever, the time to be holding her close to my side.
Now our slumbers are deep, and cool is the air of the morning,
    Now the clear song of the birds rises from delicate throats.
Dawdle a while, Aurora, unwelcome to girls and their lovers;
    Let your rosy hand take a firm grip on the reins.
Mariners read the stars better before you have risen,
    Unconfused and sure, riding the midst of the waves.
Reveille sounds at your coming: the soldier buckles his armor;
    Weary wayfaring men shoulder their burdens again.
You are the first to see farmers at work with the mattock;
    You are the first to call the slow steers under the yoke;
You cheat schoolboys of sleep, and turn them over to teachers,
    Holding their poor little hands out for the smack of the rule.
You bring many to court, witnesses, judges, and lawyers,
    Where a single word ruins many a case.
Little joy do you bring to either attorney or student,
    Each of them has to rise, starting all over each day.
You, when women might rest from the toilsome spinning and weav-
      ing,
    Call the hand to the wool, never allow them a pause.
I could endure all that—but to make girls get up in the morning,
    Who but a man with no girl ever could stand this at all?
How many times have I prayed that the wind would shatter an axle,
    Prayed for a thickening cloud, causing your horses to fall!
Hateful one, dawdle a while. Your son has come by his color
    Honestly, that we know; the heart of his mother is black.
If Tithonus would tell what he knows, no goddess in heaven

Ever deserved more blame; you flee him because he is old,
But if you held in your arms the form of the mortal you wanted,
 Then you would cry, 'Run slowly, slowly, horses of night!'
Is it my fault as a lover, if yours is old and disgusting?
 Is it my fault that you married this tiresome old man?
See how long a sleep Endymion knows in the moonlight—
 Is the moon less fair than the dawn, less beholden to love?
Jupiter doubled the nights, once, to see you less often,
 Doubling his pleasure so—Hercules' mother would know!"
So, I ended my scolding. You could tell she had heard; she was blush-
  ing.
 Nevertheless, the day came in promptly on time.

XIV

I told you, "Stop drugging your hair!"—I told you so often.
 Now you see what you get; you have no hair to be dyed.
If you had listened to me, what would you have more abundant?
 Oh, it was beautiful once, falling almost to your knee!
Yes, and delicate, too, spun gauze, like the veils of the Seres,
 Fine as the gossamer webs woven across a green lawn,
Neither blonde nor brunette, but a blending of both of those colors,
 Fusion of light and dark, gleaming like Ida's trees,
Hair that was well-behaved, and suited to hundreds of fashions,
 Never causing you pain, whether from hairpin or comb.
More than once I have watched, when the hairdresser came to at-
  tend you;
 Never, in all that time, heard the cry "Stop it! That hurts!"
Often, with hair still down, you would lie on your bed in the morn-
  ing,
 Hardly more than awake, stretched on the crimson spread;
Even in negligee, you looked like a Thracian Bacchante
 After the reel and rout relaxed in the green of a glade.
Delicate, fine, and soft as swan's-down ever, or peach-bloom,

Still, what torture that hair had to bear and endure!
Iron and fire, the brand—but they called it a curling iron:
    I protested in vain, crying out "Leave it alone!
Hardhearted girl that you are, don't you know it's a crime to be
       burning
    Hair as lovely as that, hair with a natural wave?
Take the damn iron away, put it down, throw it out, and forget it!"
    Nobody listened. Poor curls, trying to shrink from the heat!
Now they are gone, they are gone, the lovely curls that Apollo
    Or the Lord of the Vine well might wish for their own.
Why do you grieve for the loss, silly girl? Why put down your mir-
    ror,
    Shaking your head with a sigh over the beauty gone by?
So, you gaze at yourself with eyes still unused to this horror;
    If you're transfixed by it now, better forget what you were.
No enchanted herbs of a rival have done you this damage,
    No Thessalian crone sprinkled insidious bane,
Nor has illness—knock wood!—nor the tongue of the envious hurt
    you,
    No one to blame but yourself: didn't I tell you so?
Germany now will be sending the hair of her captive women
    For your adornment and grace, spoil from the conquered tribes.
People will look at your hair, and you will blush and be thinking
    "My crowning glory is now only something I bought;
They are not praising me, but some Sugambrian woman,
    Though I remember well when my pride was my own."
Ah, what a wretch I am! She is crying, hiding her blushes,
    Trying to hide them, at least, lifting a hand to her face.
She has her old curls in her lap, and stares at them, looking and
       longing—
    What in the world made her think they would be something to
       save?
Make up your mind, my dear—and make up your face! It's not fatal.
    Not very long, pretty soon, you will have hair of your own.

XV

Why, biting Envy, rant and rail at me
Calling my song the work of idle wit?
What strength I have is not for soldiery,
Nor yet for briefs or torts or wordy writ.
What you require is mortal, but my quest
Is more than that, to be forever known
Through all the world, poet and singer, blessed
With monument more durable than stone.

As long as Simois flows, or to the sky
Mount Ida towers, Homer will remain,
And Hesiod of Ascra cannot die
While the grape swells, or Ceres reaps her grain.
Renowned no more for genius than for art,
Callimachus compels the human heart.

No loss shall ever come to Sophocles;
With sun and moon Aratus' fame is sure.
Harsh fathers, bawds, sly slaves, and tarts—while these
Are with us still, Menander will endure.
And I can mention Romans with a claim
On greatness: our blunt Ennius; the high
Spirit of Accius; and Varro's fame.
When earth is dead, then will these poets die

And with them Gallus and Tibullus go,
Those gentle singers, known from East to West,
And lofty-souled Lucretius, whom we know
With Virgil, for our greatest and our best:
"Arms and the Man" may well outlive the hour
Of Rome's imperial majesty and power.

So, when the hardest iron turns to rust,
And plough and ploughshare crumble into loam,
The songs are still immortal. Monarchs must
Yield to their triumph, Portugal and Rome
Pay homage, all the gold of Araby
Be tribute due: princes and kings, bow down.
Cheap stuff may please the vulgar; as for me,
My lord Apollo, let the laurel crown

Be mine to wear; from the pure fountain pour
The water for my thirst; let lovers find
Some pleasure in me. Envy stirs no more
Once men to dust and ashes are consigned.
Still, I shall live after my final breath
And a great part of me survive my death.

BOOK

II

I

Here is another book, and Ovid again is the author,
　　Watery Sulmo's son, singing his rascally ways.
This, too, was ordered by Love. Begone, begone, O ye prudish!
　　You're not the kind of girls fit for my delicate lays.
Let me be read by a wench not cold at the sight of a lover,
　　Let me be read by the boy so far untutored in joy.
Maybe somewhere a youth, who carries the same wounds as I do,
　　Reading my lines, will find proof of the flame that he knows,
Wonder, and say to himself: "Who in the world could have told
　　him?
　　Where in the world did he learn all about me and my woes?"
I had dared, I recall, to sing of the battles in Heaven
　　(Pretty good I was, too), all about Gyas's hands,
The ill-timed vengeance of Earth, and Pelion piled upon Ossa,
　　All the towering threats offered the home of the gods.
I held there in my hands the storm clouds, Jupiter, lightning,
　　Waiting its time to be hurled for the relief of the world.
Somebody slammed a door!—and I let go of the lightning,
　　I let Jupiter down—somebody slammed a door!
Jupiter, pardon me—but how could your weapons avail me?

Thunderbolt, slam of the door—which was the deadlier shock?
Back to my own old arms, the light and flattering verses;
    Lines that smoothly run open the portals of stone.
Song brings down the horns of the blood-red moon from the heav-
        ens,
    Snow-white steeds of the sun turn again for the song,
Song breaks dragons' teeth and robs the vipers of poison,
    Song makes rivers flow rushing back to their source.
Song breaks down all doors, and barriers, harder than iron,
    Soften, keys unlock, hinges turn for a song.
What would Atreus' sons, Who's-it and What-do-you-call-him,
    Ever have done for me? What would Achilles have done?
What would I get from poor Hector, dragged by Haemonian horses?
    What from that vagabond scamp, taking ten years to get home?
But a beautiful girl, if I praise her devoutly—and often—
    Comes to the poet herself, proper reward for the song.
Who wants anything more? Farewell, illustrious heroes!
    What you have to supply isn't the portion for me.
Pretty ones, turn your heads, and watch me while I am singing
    Prompted by rosy Love; pretty ones, listen a while.

II

Listen, Bagoas: I know you're supposed to be guarding the lady.
    Just a few words in your ear, brief and straight to the point.
Yesterday afternoon, near the portico of Apollo
    New on the Palatine Hill, I saw her taking a stroll;
Saw her, wanted her, wrote her, sent the letter, and asked her.
    Back, in a shaky hand, came the answer: "I can't!"
"But why can't you?", I asked, and then she told me the reason.
    You were the reason, my friend, you and your vigilant guard.
If you have any sense, you had better stop meriting hatred;
    Men who are fearful desire death for the object they fear.
And her husband's a fool: why take such pains to be guarding

Stuff that without a guard really would suffer no harm?
Let him (he's crazy, of course) persist in his foolish delusion:
     Even if many admire, isn't she perfectly pure?
Give her a little freedom—what are a few stolen moments?
     Any indulgence you give she will be glad to repay.
If you aid and abet, the mistress is bound to the servant;
     If you fear to conspire, can't you at least close your eyes?
So, if she's reading a letter, assume that it came from her mother;
     If a stranger arrives, you thought he was some one you know.
If she tells you her best friend is sick, though you're sure she is per-
          fectly healthy
     She's dying, for all you know: what do you care? Let her go.
If she is late coming home, don't tire yourself out with long waiting;
     When she comes in at the door, give a resounding snore.
Never you mind what goes on at the temple of linen-robed Isis,
     In the theater-stall—pay no attention at all.
If you know what she does, convert it to honor, and profit:
     Where was there easier work, ever, than shutting the mouth?
Blows do not fall on the slave endowed with the gift of discretion;
     He can be lord in the house, the others, abject, at his feet.
Make up a few good lies to tell, in a pinch, to her husband;
     Both will appear to approve; only one actually will.
After he's wrinkled his brow, put on a big act with his scowling,
     What, in the end, does he do? Just what she wanted him to.
Once in a while, let her scold you, let her pretend to be crying,
     Call you all kinds of bad names, a hangman, a monster, a beast.
You answer back and upbraid her for things she'll explain away
          safely.
     When accusations are false, true ones may not be believed.
So your credit will grow, and so will your cash, into savings:
     Do as I tell you, and soon you will be perfectly free.
Tattletales wear on their necks collars of iron—you've noticed?—
     Servants disloyal, untrue, eat out their hearts in the gaol.
Tantalus reaches for fruit, for the water that always escapes him:

That was the price he paid for his too garrulous tongue.
Little was Argo preserved by his zealous watch over Io;
   Io's a goddess now, Argus gone to his grave.
I saw a fellow once, his legs half rotting in shackles.
   What was his crime? He told someone his wife was untrue.
He deserved worse than he got, for his tongue hurt both by its
     malice—
   Husband in anguish and wife put to unbearable shame.
Accusations, believe me, never delight any husband:
   Maybe he'll listen, but still—how do they help him at all?
If he's lukewarm, doesn't care, you will waste time with your gabble;
   If he burns up, poor wretch, you'll only make him feel worse.
Nothing is easy to prove: though you catch her, *flagrante delicto*,
   Somehow she gets off safe; cuckolded justice is blind.
He may have seen her himself, and yet he'll believe her denials,
   Doubt his very own eyes, prove to himself that he lies.
Let him look at her tears, and soon he'll be sobbing, and roaring
   "You'll get in trouble for this!"—What did you think he would
     say?
Why sit in on the game when the odds are not in your favor?
   You'll take a beating, while she smiles from the lap of her judge.
It's no crime we are planning; we are not getting together
   To compound poisonous brews, to flash the sword in our hand;
All we are asking of you is a chance for some safety in loving:
   What in the world could there be any more easy to give?

III

Poor castrate chaperon, I suffer too
Since you, who guard the lady, cannot have
The joys of love. The man who altered you
Deserved, himself, to take the wounds he gave.
You would be more compliant to my pleading
If love for woman ever made you hot.

Unfit for warlike spear or feats of riding
What all (or most) men have, those you have not.

So fetch and carry for her, be a bar
To youth, and beauty's amorous intent.
She still could fool you, nuisance though you are:
What two have willed lacks not accomplishment.
Since nothing can be lost by courtesies,
Pro tempore, I'm asking—Mister, please!

IV

I would not dare to defend my absolute absence of morals;
    I would not smother my faults under a blanket of lies.
No: I own up; I confess, if any confession can help me;
    Wailing *My grievous fault*, how I lash out at my sins!
I hate what I am, and yet, for all my desiring,
    Cannot be anything else—what a misfortune to bear!
Borne along like a ship tossed on tempestuous waters,
    Out of control, I lack will power to keep me aright.
There is no definite One whose beauty drives me to frenzy;
    No: there are hundreds, almost, keeping me always in love.
If there's a modest one, whose eyes are always cast downward,
    I am on fire, in a snare, set by her innocent ways.
If one is forward and brash, I rejoice that she's not country-simple;
    I foresee quite a romp, bouncing around in her bed.
If she seems cold and austere, behaving like one of the Sabines,
    I suspect that she craves more than she's willing to show.
If she has read any books, I am overwhelmed by her culture;
    Never read one in her life?—that makes her sweet and un-
        spoiled.
One of them says my songs make a boor of Callimachus—surely,
    There's the critic for me; any admirer I love.
Somebody else comes along, sure of one thing, I'm no poet;

Wouldn't it be a delight to lay her objections to rest?
One steps soft, and I love the way she moves; and another
    Is hard, but the touch of a man might make her melt in your
      arms.
One sings beautiful songs, and one plays beautiful music—
    Kiss the mouth of one, hold the other one's hands!
One is a dancer, swaying, the perfect picture of rhythm,
    Movements luring my heart with the seduction of art.
Let Hippolytus stand in my shoes, and adopt my demeanor—
    Straightway before your eyes what a Priapus will rise!
That one is tall and a peer of the epic daughters of heroes—
    Wonderful sight to behold, lying full length on a bed!
This one is cunning, and short, and I am the victim of either;
    Whether they're tall or short, both suit the wish of my heart.
One does not dress very well—imagine her fitted by Dior!
    One is stunningly gowned—think of her negligee!
Redheads, or blondes, or brunettes, no matter; I'm theirs for the
    taking.
    Dark complexion or fair, I'm not the fellow to care.
Dusky tresses and neck snow-white—why, that could be Leda!
    Golden, shot with bronze fire—that was Aurora's appeal.
All of the legends there are, translations, original sources,
    I can adapt to my love, put any version to use.
Fresh ones (not legends, but girls) and older ones also attract me,
    These by mature *savoir-faire*, those by endearing young charms.
All-embracing, I think, is the proper term for my passion;
    There's not a sweetheart in town I'd be reluctant to love.

V

Cupid, be gone with your quiver! No love is worth so much trouble
    That with my every breath I keep on praying for death.
Death's what I'm praying for, though, when I think that you have
    betrayed me.

What a creature you are, making me wretched for life!
No intercepted note has told me of what you've been doing;
    No gift secretly sent given your cheating away.
Would that my case were so weak no court in the world would sus-
        tain it!
    Wretch that I am, alas! Why must my case be so strong?
Lucky the man who can venture a bold defense of his loved one,
    Lucky the man whom she tells, "I didn't do it!" (If true.)
Made of iron, or mad, or a masochist, no doubt about it,
    Such is the fellow who craves proof beyond shadow of doubt.
But I saw you, I say, and I was perfectly sober,
    Though I know what you thought—I was both drunk and
        asleep.
I was watching you both, I saw you waving your eyebrows;
    I could tell what you said when you were nodding your head.
And your eyes were not dumb, nor the scribbles you made on the
        table,
    Dipping your fingers in wine, each of the letters a sign.
Oh, and the double-talk, too, under the innocent meanings,
    Messages broadcast in code—don't think I misunderstood.
Well, the party broke up, and most of the guests had departed,
    Maybe a sleeper or so too saturated to go.
I saw you kiss him; I knew tongues were involved in the kissing,
    Never a doubt in my mind; that was no sisterly buss.
That was the way a girl responds, when she and her lover
    Both are eager and hot, both unable to wait.
Not the kind of a kiss Diana might offer Apollo,
    More like Venus and Mars, almost unlimited times.
"What are you doing?" I scream, "Why are you giving another
    Joys that are properly mine? This I will never endure!
We have the right to kiss that way, we belong to each other,
    But for a third to intrude—isn't that just a bit crude?"
That's what I said, and some more, with words dictated by anger.
    She was aware of her guilt; over her face came a blush

Like the sky grown red with the hues of Aurora at morning,
> Like a bride's when the groom comes the first time to their
> room;
So do roses glow, when intermingled with lilies;
> So does the white of the moon color when caught by the sun.
Like one of these, very much, she blushed, and her blushing was
> lovely.
> Never in all her life was she more fair to behold.
She kept her eyes on the ground, and keeping them there was be-
> coming;
> There was grief in her gaze, grief of a beautiful kind.
Even so, I was wild, ready to give her a slapping,
> Ready to yank at her hair, snarl that impressive *coiffure.*
But when I looked at her face, my arms hung limp from my shoul-
> ders:
> She had arms of her own, much more effective than mine.
I, who was recently wild, was humble now, and a pleader,
> Kisses I begged her for, kisses more ardent than those.
Smiling, she gave me her best, with a fervor and force that would
> make Jove,
> At the height of his rage, let his thunderbolt fall.
I was tormented again, because my rival had tasted,
> Probably, kisses as sweet, possibly, even much more.
These were better, it seemed, by far than the ones I had taught her;
> Something seemed to be gained, something surprisingly new.
Not a good sign, or too good, for all of her tongue to be searching,
> Working around in my mouth, taking all mine into hers.
I don't exactly complain of this particular feature;
> Still, I have one complaint (if I have any at all):
Only in bed could she get instruction in this kind of kissing.
> Who was her tutor, and when? What did he get for his pay?

47

VI

So, the parrot is dead, that mimicking bird from the Indies.
    Come, all ye faithful birds, come to his funeral rites.
Beat your breasts with your wings, and claw your cheeks with your
        talons,
    Let your plumage be torn, wail your most desolate songs!
Why, Philomela, complain of the old Ismarian outrage?
    That is a grief outworn, dulled by the passage of time.
Turn to the sorry fate of a bird quite out of the common;
    Sorrow for Itys no more; that is a grief of the past.
All you birds, who hover and poise and balance in clear air,
    You more than all the rest, affable turtledove, mourn.
All your life together was harmony, blessed devotion;
    Damon and Pythias knew fellowship such as you two.
Yet what availed that *rapport*, or the rare and beautiful color?
    What availed that voice, expert in mimicking speech?
What availed it to please my girl as soon as she saw you?
    Glory of birds, alas! now you lie fallen and low.
Ah, but the green of your wings outshone the emerald's luster,
    Rubies and jasper were dim to the red and gold of your beak.
Never, in all the world, such a bird who could imitate talking,
    Reproducing, exact, all of the tones of the voice.
Envy has taken you off—you were no mover of warfare,
    You were a lover of peace, mild in your chattering talk.
Quails will bicker and brawl, and some folks say that's the reason
    They, like harridan crones, live to a ripe old age.
You were content with a little, a very little, and eating
    Seemed like a waste of time better devoted to speech.
You could make do with a nut, or some poppy seeds taken at bed-
        time;
    Water, perfectly pure, sated your innocent thirst.
Still the gluttonous vulture survives, and the kite wheels in circles,
    Still the jackdaw survives, certain foreteller of rain,

Still the raven is left, hateful to armored Minerva,
    A bird with more lives than a cat, nine generations at least.
All of them still live on, but the talkative parrot has perished,
    Gone with the gift of his voice, brought from the end of the
        world.
Almost always the best, it seems, are the first to be taken:
    Envy permits to the worse fuller completion of days.
Protesilaus fell; who attended his last rites? Thersites.
    Hector was ashes and dust; Priam and Paris lived on.
Why should I mention the anxious prayers of my dearly beloved,
    Vows in devotion made, lost on the southerly gales?
Your seventh day drew nigh, with no successor attending;
    Fate loomed over your head, the skein of your life was unwound,
Yet your faltering strength resisted the garroting silence,
    What were your dying words? Only, "Corinna, farewell!"
Under a hill in Elysium, a grove, dark-green with the holm-oak,
    Blooms, and the grass on the ground shines with perpetual
        green.
That is the place, we are told, if skeptics can ever believe it,
    Where all good birds go, evil ones never aspire.
There the innocent swans rejoice in the greenest of meadows,
    There the phoenix lives on, only bird of his kind,
There the peacock of Juno, forever displaying her glories,
    Dwells, and the turtledove kisses her amorous mate.
There will our parrot come, to a home in Elysian woodlands,
    Charming all faithful birds, drawn to his talent with words.
Over his bones will rise a tomb, of seemly proportion,
    Where a modest stone still has room for a verse:
"This memorial proves how dear I was to my lady,
    I, who in skill of speech greatly excelled any bird."

VII

Am I forever to be put on trial?
Grant that I win, I tire of winning cases.
If I turn round, what use is my denial
That I am not in search of pretty faces?
Or if a lovely girl goes walking by
And never says a word, at once you claim
That I am really giving her the eye.
I'm just as guilty if I praise, or blame.

Are my cheeks ruddy? Then you call me cold.
Pale? Then you say another wears me out.
I wish to God that I had kissed, and told,
Given you something to complain about,
But as things are, your credulous invective
Becomes both wearisome, and ineffective.

Now a new charge! Cypassis, so you say,
The girl who sets your hair, allegedly
Enjoyed with me a tumble in the hay,
In plainer English, went to bed with me.
Ye gods! If any such intent were mine,
Could I find pleasure in a servile slut?
What man, born free, would ever want to twine
His arms around a waist the lash has cut?

Moreover, she's supposed to fix your curls,
Furnish you service, a devoted maid,
A fine one to seduce, of all the girls!
What for?—to be refused, and then betrayed?
I swear, by wingèd Cupid and his bow,
By Venus, too—it simply isn't so.

VIII

Adept in all the ways of setting hair,
Cypassis, and accomplished in the lore
Of other arts involving *savoir-faire*,
You suit Corinna, but you suit me more.
But who, what tattletale, I want to know,
Told her that we were cheating on the side?
Have I been blushing, made some *gaffe*, to show,
To give away what we had planned to hide?

Suppose I did say one who loved a slave
Must be a half-wit: Agamemnon fell
For Phoebas; and the great Achilles gave
His heart and manhood over to the spell
Of golden Briseis. What kings approved
Why should I find unworthy to be loved?

But when she fixed on you her angry frown,
You blushed, I saw you. I had more control,
If you remember; I swore up and down
That I was faithful, perjuring my soul.
Venus, forgive me; let the south wind sweep
The lies—they were a gentleman's—away,
And you, my dark beloved, shall we sleep
Tonight, together? I deserve my pay.

Why do you shake your head, as if in fright,
Ungrateful girl? How stupid can you be?
If you refuse me, I will go tonight,
I'll be the one, myself, to tell on me,
Giving her every detail of our crimes,
Where, when, what methods, and how many times.

IX

O Cupid, never roused enough for me,
Idle and worthless lodger in my heart,
Why hurt me for my loyal soldiery
With wounds—in my own camp!—that burn and smart?
Why burn the torch, or bend the bow, at friends?
'Twere greater glory to subdue a foe.
Did not the great Achilles make amends,
Healing the victim whom his spear laid low?

Good huntsmen follow only fleeing game,
Leave taken quarry for the bird that flies.
Your arms oppress us, meek, abject, and tame;
Against a foe your hand is slow to rise.
Why blunt the barbs on flesh that might be stone,
Now love has stripped me to the very bone?

So many men still sleep alone, ungirled:
In that direction let your triumph draw.
Had Rome not loosed her might against the world,
She'd be, not gold nor marble now, but straw.
Old soldiers, their long term of service over,
Retire to acres given by the state,
And an old race horse kicks his heels in clover
When he is done with breaking from the gate.

Long docks hide vessels weary of the wave,
The sword is sheathed, the cries of battle cease.
An old campaigner with the girls, I gave
Good service in those wars; so now for peace.
Yet, should the god say, "Granted!" I'd protest;
Too sweet a trouble, this, to change for rest.

When I am surfeited, and ardor dies,
Then truly I am wretched, whirled in vain,
A rider on a frenzied horse, that flies
Fighting, hardmouthed, against the bit and rein,
A vessel, almost safe, in sight of land,
Is taken thus, by gale and ocean-swell.
So Cupid's veering pleasure takes command,
Bright love resumes the weapons I know well.

Transfix me, boy; I offer no defense,
An easy target, a familiar mark,
Your arrows know me for their residence
More than your quiver, even in the dark.
As for the man who sleeps all through the night
And calls his slumbers blest—God help his plight!

For, stupid, what is sleep but cold death's twin?
The fates will give us ample time for rest.
What if a lying sweetheart takes me in?
Expectancy is rapture in the breast.
Let her talk sweetly, let her rail and shout,
Let me enjoy her, or come beaten back.
Mars is a most capricious god, no doubt;
Why not, with Cupid schooling his attack?

For you are lighter, Cupid, more impelled
By wind than your frail wings, and all the joy
You give is taken back, held forth, withheld,
Yet—here's my heart for kingdom, wingèd boy!
Reign here, and all the girls will flock about,
A fickle congregation, but devout.

X

You were the one, Graecinus—oh, yes, you certainly told me
    No one on earth could love more than one girl at a time.
That was a lie; it's your fault that I am completely defenseless;
    I admit it with shame—I love two at a time.
Both are beautiful girls, and both of them elegant dressers,
    Which is better in bed, that I confess I don't know.
One has the prettier looks, but sometimes I think it's the other;
    Each of them pleases me more—what is a fellow to do?
Like a yacht, or a yawl, with the winds from opposite quarters,
    I keep veering about, driven now this way, now that.
Why do you double my trouble, O Venus, O Lady of Eryx?
    Wasn't one girl, one alone, plenty to have on my mind?
Why add leaves to the trees, or stars to the constellations?
    Why bring waters and floods, pouring them into the seas?
Still, it is better this way than lying unloved and forsaken;
    Let my enemies have the lot of the Puritan life.
Let my enemies sleep alone, under desolate covers,
    Let them have plenty of room when they turn over in bed!
But as for me, let love break off my sleep, be demanding,
    Be insistent, and I never the one to deny.
Let my girl wear me out, and no one say *No!* to us, either.
    One may suffice; if not, where's the objection to two?
I can make out well enough—my limbs are slender, but able;
    I am all nerve, not bulk; what good rooster is fat?
Pleasure will add to my strength, my potent reserve, and my prow-
      ess:
    Show me the girl who can say I couldn't answer her need.
More than once in the night I have risen to every occasion,
    Risen, again at dawn, a thoroughly competent man.
Lucky the man who dies in duels with Venus as second.
    Grant me, gods, such an end, if I must die in my bed.
Let the soldier expose his breast to the darts of the foeman,

Let his crimson blood buy him a glorious name,
Let the trader seek wealth, and die in the midst of a shipwreck,
     Thirsting for more than gain, drinking the salt of the sea.
But as for me, let me go in the act of coming to Venus;
     In more senses than one, let my last dying be done.
And at my funeral rites, let one of the mourners bear witness:
     "That was the way, we know, he would have wanted to go."

XI

All this evil began when the pine-tree from Pelion's summit
     First taught wondering waves how men could travel the sea,
And the reckless ship, which the Clashing Rocks never damaged,
     Steered its way home again, bearing the Golden Fleece.
Would that the *Argo* had sunk and tasted the waters of shipwreck,
     Warning all men that the oar never should trouble the main.
Now Corinna prepares to venture those treacherous pathways,
     Leaving her household gods, leaving the couch that she knows.
Wretch that I am, for her sake I shall dread every wind of the ocean,
     West wind, East wind, North, even the balm-laden South.
There you will find no wonderful towns, no marvelous forests,
     Only the dark-blue deep, only the pitiless sea.
Nor does that sea, far out, hold shells and bright-colored pebbles;
     Those we must find near home, strolling the edge of the sand.
Print on the strand the trace of your marble-white feet, O ye
     maidens!
     So far the way is safe, all of the rest of it blind.
Let others tell you the tales of Scylla and dreadful Charybdis,
     All of the wars of the waves taking the shock of the wind;
Let them tell you about the sheer Ceraunian rock-falls,
     Tell where the Quicksands lurk, lying in wait for their prey.
Learn about these from the rest, and believe whatever they tell you;
     If you believe them enough, storm-winds can bring you no
     harm.

Once the cable is loosed, and the prow cuts the fathomless ocean,
    Then it is all too late, watching, regretting the land;
When the sailor, in dread, shudders at boisterous storm-winds,
    Noting that death is as near as the water under the keel.
What if Triton's blast should shake the ocean to fury?
    All your color would leave, white as the foam of the wave.
Then let Nereus make the ocean a down-hill highway;
    Crying, "Happy the girl held in her own native land!"
Safer—too late for it now—to keep your bed warm, or be reading
    All of your books, or strum, idly, the Orphean lyre.
Yet, if the scud of the gale must sweep all my wishes to nothing,
    May Galatea be kind, granting you haven and calm.
Nereus, yours be the blame, yours and all of your daughters,
    If such a girl is lost, wrecked on some desolate coast.
Think of me as you go; invoke a wind for returning,
    One that will speed you home, swelling the full of the sail.
Then let Nereus make the ocean a down-hill highway;
    Blow her home to me, wind; rush her home to me, tide.
Pray, my dear, yourself, for the winds to billow the canvas;
    Lay your hand on the sails; they will swell at your touch.
Let me be first, where I stand on the shore, to catch sight of the
        vessel,
    Telling myself "That ship carries my idol back home."
I will take you in my arms and kiss you times without number,
    And the victim will fall, vowed for your safe return.
The sand will be smoothed, somehow, levelled off, for a couch to
        recline on,
    Some sort of mound be raised, making a table for two.
There, when the wine is poured, you will tell me about your adven-
        tures,
    How the ship, outbound, almost went down in the waves,
How, when you hastened to me, you feared no evil in darkness,
    Feared no blast of the wind roaring out of the south.
I will believe it all, though every bit may be fiction—

56

Why should I not believe flatteries dear to my heart?
Oh, may the Morning-star, most brilliant of all in the heaven,
    Race his loose-reined steed, hurry that moment to me!

XII

Now let triumphant laurels crown my brow!
We've won; here in my arms Corinna lies.
No husbands, guardians, hostile doors can now
Prevail, defraud me of my lovely prize.
And what a signal victory: all hail,
Great strategist, by whom no blood was shed,
No walls assailed, no warriors clad in mail,
Only a girl brought peaceably to bed.

When, after ten long years, tall Troy came down,
Part of the glory went to Atreus' son,
But I admit no allies in renown,
I was my army, a victorious one,
Commander, captain, standard-bearer, knight,
And first-class private on the field of fight.

Luck had no part in this; it all was planned.
Nor do I claim original pretext.
Who but a woman set the Lapith band
To fight with Centaurs drunk and over-sexed?
Europe and Asia never would have warred
Had Helen not been taken; yet once more
Trojans were sent to battle for their lord
Over a woman, on Latinus' shore.

Forget the Sabine brides—not men alone
Compete for females; bulls, for instance, bawl
And snort and charge and stand a shock, like stone,

For some white heifer, witness of it all.
My victories were bloodless, Cupid knows,
Greatest of all generalissimos!

XIII

Corinna, having tried, with her own hand,
To cure herself of pregnancy, lies low.
I should be angry at the deed she planned,
The risk she took, and never let me know.
But anger yields to fear—I was the cause,
At least, I might have been; the chance was there.
Since *posse* may be *esse*, if I was,
O Isis, bring us comfort, hear my prayer!

Come from Canopus, Pharos rich in palms,
Where seven-mouthed Nile moves gliding to the sea,
Osiris speed you here, with healing balms,
Give life to her, and so give life to me.
She never failed your services beside
Those laurels where the Gallic horsemen ride.

And you, Birth-Goddess, pitying the dole
Of women in long labor, great with child,
Hear the entreaties of an anguished soul,
Have pity on her, merciful and mild!
Favor my prayers, and intercede for her—
She is not all unworthy of your grace—
And I, white-robed, will be your minister,
Bring you due gifts, in proper time and place.

And more than that—by my own hand engraved
A verse upon a votive stone will read
"Ovid is grateful for Corinna saved,"

Memorial in word as well as need.
Frightened, and tactless, like so many men,
I add, "Corinna, don't do this again!"

XIV

How does it help the girls to be free of the burdens of warfare,
Unlike Amazon hosts, following fierce in the fray,
If, without peril of war, they wound themselves with their weapons,
Make their unseeing hands instruments furthering death?
She who first made bold to take new life from her body
Should have perished herself, taking the death that she gave.
If the mothers of old had followed so vicious a custom,
All of the human race would have been gone from the world,
Or a new couple be found, to throw, like Deucalion and Pyrrha,
Over unpeopled plains, life in the form of the stones.
Who would have shattered the wealth of Troy, had beautiful Thetis
Not submitted to bear the burden of Peleus' son?
Ilia, had she slain the twins in her womb, would have murdered
Founders and city alike, murdered imperial Rome.
What if Anchises' seed had been aborted by Venus,
Then what of Arms and the Man? where would our Caesars
have been?
You yourself would have died, and all of your loveliness wasted
If your mother had tried any such trick as you played,
And what would have happened to me, had mine gone in for abortions,
Cheating me out of my chance, some day, of dying for love?
Why defraud the vine, full-grown, of the ripening clusters?
Why let the cruel hand ravage the blossom in bud?
Ripeness is all. Let things unborn develop and quicken:
Only a little delay; life is a splendid reward.
Women, why dig at yourselves with instruments probing your vitals?
Why do you poison new lives even before they are born?

Don't hold out, as excuse, the crimes of Medea and Procris,
    Women who murdered their sons, tragic in passionate rage:
They could claim motive at least, their wicked, perfidious husbands;
    Who is this Tereus, pray? who has been Jasoning you?
Tigresses wouldn't do this, in the darkest Armenian jungles,
    Nor would the lion's mate ever perform such a deed.
Only the girls do this, the tenderhearted, the darlings,
    Not with impunity, though; sometimes the slayers are slain.
So they are borne to the pyre, their hair unloosened, and people
    Cry, "Deservedly so!" while the procession goes by.
May these words of mine be swept away to the heavens,
    Solemn pronouncements of mine be without ominous sign.
Merciful gods, this once let her get away with it safely,
    If she is guilty again, let her atone for her sin.

XV

Worthless, except as token that might prove
The giver's love, go, little ring, to find
The proper finger of my lady love!
Let her accept you with a happy mind.
May you fit her as well as she fits me:
With symbol of the circle, hold and cling.
Already I am envious to see
How close to her you are; O lucky ring!

Would that, by Circe's or by Proteus' art,
I might become at once this gift of mine,
And on her finger touch, almost, her heart,
Be thrust inside her dress by her design
And there, however close and clinging, stir
From finger-tip to search for more of her.

Or, to help seal her letters, when the dry
Jewel might clog with clinging wax, and stain,

I'd take the moisture from her lips, but I
Would seal no missive that might cause me pain.
Entrust me to the casket?—Never so!
I would hold tight, resist, contract and clutch,
With every artifice refuse to go,
And yet—I would not burden her too much.

Wear me when bathing—water will not harm
The hardness of the jewel, though the sight
Of all your naked and exciting charm
Could change my round to straight; indeed, it might.
What foolishness; Go, little ring, to her
As love's ambassador and minister.

XVI

I am in Sulmo now, out in Paelignian country,
    No great place, but the streams make it a health-giving land.
Though the sun cracks the earth with the merciless flood of his
        power,
    Though the Dog-star burns fierce with the blaze of his fire,
Through the Paelignian fields wander the clear-flowing waters;
    There the grass grows green out of luxurious loam.
The acres are rich in corn and richer in fruit of the vineyards;
    Here and there you can find silvery olive-groves.
Meadows are green and brooks divide the green of the meadows;
    Turf is almost a shade over the dampness of ground.
Here my fire burns not. Hold it a moment—correction!
    She who kindles my fire is away, but the fire does burn.
I would not like it in Heaven, with Castor and Pollux beside me;
    Were you not at my side, Heaven to me would be Hell.
May they toss in their graves and the clay rest heavy upon them,
    Those designers of roads, those highway engineers!
Or, if roads had to be cut, and the earth be furrowed by turnpikes,

There should have been a law: Travel forbidden to One.
Then, if I shivered my way over the Dolomite summits,
Travel would not be too cold, knowing your warmth at my side,
Neither, with you at my side, would I quail at the Libyan quick-
sands,
Driving my ship full-sail toward the ill-omening south.
I, with you at my side, would sneer at Charybdis and Scylla,
Face with resolute heart Malea's merciless wave.
If our vessel went down, with our mascots conquered by Neptune,
If the violent gods carried our lifeboats away,
Twine your snow-white arms around the neck of your lover,
I would bear you along, easily breasting the wave.
Look at Leander, who swam the straits to be with his darling;
Only once did he fail, lost in the blindness of night.
Here without you, though the vines are busy with men at their labor,
Though the rivers brim up to the verge of the field,
Though the countryman dares ripples to swell into currents,
Though the cool of the breeze stirs in the top of the trees,
I do not seem to be in the healthful Paelignian country,
Not in my native land, not on my father's ground,
But in Russia, or worse, in the midst of the blue-painted Britons,
Bound to horrible rocks, red with Promethean gore.
The elm is in love with the vine: the vine keeps faith with the elm-
tree;
Why should I always be torn from the desire of my heart?
Yet you had sworn you would be my companion, always beside me;
That you swore by the stars, or by the light of your eyes.
Woman's words are as light as the doomed leaves whirling in au-
tumn,
Easily swept by the wind, easily drowned by the wave.
If there is still in your heart some feeling of faith toward a lost man,
Add to the promise you made something by way of a deed.
Soon as you can, shake the reins over the manes of your ponies,
Whirl the light car along, swiftly as ever you can,

And, wherever she comes, O hills, sink low for her passing,
    O be easy to ride, winding roads in the vales!

XVII

If anyone thinks it a shame to be the slave of a woman,
    With such a person as judge, I am convicted of shame.
I will accept the disgrace, if the fires would only burn lower!
    Venus, born of the waves, Cyprian, hear my appeal!
Would I had fallen, as prey, to some one a little bit gentler;
    Prey to a beautiful one I was intended to be.
Loveliness makes women proud: Corinna knows she is lovely.
    Wretch that I am, her pride makes her disdainful of me.
Why does she know herself well? Because she looks in her mirror;
    Never looks into it, though, till she's made up for the day.
Even if pride, and good looks, give you the chance of dominion—
    O good looks that were born for the delight of my eyes!—
Even so, you should not despise me, compared to your beauty.
    Lesser things, we are told, may be adapted to great.
Even Calypso, a nymph, could fall in love with a mortal,
    Keeping Ulysses from home, where he was longing to go.
Who brought Achilles to birth? A human king, and a goddess:
    Numa, who gave us the law, married no mortal bride;
Venus shares her bed with Vulcan, ridiculous limper—
    The very meter I use shows a mismatching of feet.
Light of my life, never mind: take me, and set the conditions;
    Lay down the law to me, whether abroad or in bed.
I shall not bring you disgrace, nor will you rejoice if I leave you;
    Our kind of love will be something we must not deny.
Song is my happy estate, though I'm poor in other possessions;
    Many a girl, I have found, wants me to bring her renown.
I know one who claims that she is really Corinna:
    She would have given a lot if she could make it be true.
Cold Eurotas and Po, under the alleys of poplars,
    Far from each other glide smoothly their separate ways.

Nobody else but you will ever be sung in my verses,
    No inspiration but you tender me subject for praise.

XVIII

While you, Macer, compose lines on the wrath of Achilles,
    Dressing the chieftains, sworn, in the first armor of war,
I am dawdling around, relaxed in the shadow of Venus;
    All my ambition breaks down under the pressure of Love.
Often I've said to my girl: "Go away now! I ought to be writing."
    What does she do, right away? Comes and sits on my lap.
Often I've said, "It's disgraceful!" and she, most tearfully, answers:
    "Poor little me! So soon—now he thinks love's a disgrace."
Then she'll be throwing her arms around me, and giving me kisses,
    Thousands, I guess, I lose track, I am a poet undone.
I give in, I recall my troops from the fields they had entered;
    I sing of feats at home, sing of my private campaigns.
Ah, but the Tragic Muse, one time, engaged my attention,
    Growing in stature, too; I must admit I was good.
Only—the trouble was—Love laughed out loud at my buskins,
    Laughed at my robes and my mask, laughed at the scepter I
    bore.
Also, my girl didn't like it: between us, I think she was jealous.
    Love proceeded to chain the buskinny feet of the bard.
So, now, I write what I may, the arts of the tenderest passion,
    Often enough, I must own, practicing things that I preach,
Or I put down the words Penelope sent to Ulysses,
    Tears of Phyllis, forlorn, letters for Paris to read,
Letters for Jason, the ingrate! and others too many to mention,
    Dido, holding the sword; *Sappho, to Phaon, with love.*
And they are answered, too—another author, Sabinus,
    Poet and friend of mine, made up replies to them all.
Even in your own work, dear Macer, writer of epic,
    Golden Love can be heard through the alarums of war.

Paris and Helen are there, the adulterous and the devoted,
> Laodamia, too, faithful even in death.
Stories like these, I suspect, appeal to you better than battles;
> Soon, if I know you, you'll come out of your camp into mine.

XIX

Fool, if you feel no need to guard your girl for your own sake,
> See that you guard her for mine, so I may want her the more.
Easy things nobody wants, but what is forbidden is tempting;
> He has no heart in his breast who loves with his rival's consent.
Hope and fear should be conflicting emotions with lovers;
> Let the occasional *No!* be an incentive to vows.
What do I care for the luck that never takes trouble to fool me?
> I don't consider it love if it can't hurt me at all.
This Corinna has learned, too well, and fully exploited,
> Mistress of every device, cunning at taking me in.
How many times has she lied, about a bad headache, for instance,
> Ordering me to go home, loath as I was to be gone!
How many times has she heaped unjust accusations upon me,
> Acting as if she believed stories she knew she made up!
Then, when she has me all hot and bothered, she'll turn to an angel:
> Nothing I ask is refused—what an adorable girl!
Sweet in her winsome ways, enchanting in her endearments,
> Kissing me—Oh my God!—better not go into that.
Since you have stolen my heart, remember to be a bit cautious:
> Be on your guard against plots; often, entreated, say *No!*
Make me lie at your door, and spend the night on your threshold;
> Let me suffer the cold through the long frost of the night.
So does my love grow strong, persistent through all of the seasons.
> This is the way to help, this is the diet for love.
Love fed fat soon turns to boredom and even abhorrence;
> Too much sweetness is bad, not for the belly alone.
Danae, unconfined by the tower of bronze and its rigor,

Would not have known, in the gold, the penetration of Jove.
Juno, setting her watch over Io, changed to a heifer,
    Saw that Io became dearer in sight of her god.
If it's the easy you want, go pull down leaves from the forest,
    Take the drink of your thirst from a great river in flood.
She who desires long reign should make a fool of her lover—
    Ovid, look out! You'll be hurt by the precepts you give.
Well, never mind: I am sure I have no desire for indulgence:
    Her who follows I flee; her who runs off I pursue.
You, my rival, I fear, are becoming just a bit cocky—
    Better begin toward night checking the lock on the door,
Better begin to ask whose tread is that in the evening,
    What, in the stilly night, causes the dogs to bark,
What are those tablets her maid forever seems to be bringing,
    Why, so often, she sleeps all by herself in her bed.
Let such worries as these, once in a while, feed on your marrow;
    Give me the chance to prove I am resourceful in love.
Anyone who can love the wife of an indolent cuckold,
    I should suppose, would steal buckets of sand from the shore.
Now hear this, in time: if you don't begin to be watchful,
    She will begin, I fear, shortly to cease to be mine.
I have stood it as long as I can, have been both hopeful and patient,
    Waiting the time till you gave me a perfect excuse.
You dull oaf, you endure things that no husband should suffer:
    Such complacence will be dismissal of passion for me.
Am I to be out of luck forever, forever prevented,
    Even at night from the fear of some outrageous revenge?
Shall I fear nothing at all? never heave sighs in my slumbers?
    Will you never take steps making me wish you were dead?
What have I to do with a husband, or should I say, pander,
    With a suspicionless mind, spoiling my possible fun?
Why not seek somebody else, who would really delight in your
    patience?
    If I'm the rival you want, kindly forbid me to be.

66

BOOK

III

I

Ancient, untouched by the axe for many a year, stands the wood-
    land.
    There, you would have to believe, surely divinity dwells.
In the midst is a spring, and a cavern with rocks hanging over;
    There from every side comes the sweet song of the birds.
I was wandering there, under the arches of shadow;
    I was wondering there, which of the Muses to seek.
Elegy came, with her hair most neat and pleasantly scented;
    One of her feet, I could see, somewhat exceeded its mate.
Lovely she was, in her gossamer dress and affectionate glances;
    Even her uneven gait had an eccentric charm.
Also Tragedy came, striding with violent passion,
    Wearing a glowering look, robes that were sweeping the ground.
In her left hand she bore, and almost brandished, a scepter,
    And on her feet she wore Lydian buskins, high-bound.
She was the first to speak: "Will there be any end to this loving,
    Obdurate poet and vain, over-concerned with your theme?
People at parties discuss nothing but you and your follies;
    Even the crossroads hear tales of your follies and you.
People gesture and point as you walk through the streets of the city:

67

'There he goes; that's the one, burned by the fierceness of love.'
You are the talk of the town, though apparently you don't know it,
    Or it may be you don't care, broadcasting all your disgrace.
Is it not time to be moved by a more appropriate measure?
    Enter on greater work; quit all this fooling around.
Genius depends on the theme. Sing of the exploits of heroes,
    Here (you may say to yourself), here is the field for your art.
Up to this point your Muse has been frivolous, giving you poems
    All good enough for the girls; Ovid, it's time to grow up.
Let me become, through you, ennobled Tragedy, Roman;
    My fulfillment requires your inspiration and power."
So she spoke, tossing her head, tall in her resolute striding,
    While the other one smiled, holding a branch in her hand,
Myrtle, or could I be wrong? She spoke in answer: "You bore me,
    Tragedy, pompous and proud; why are you always a bore?
Still, you have deigned to descend, expressing yourself in my meter;
    In your quarrel with me, still you make use of my strains.
I would not dare to pretend that I can equal your diction—
    Portals as lofty as yours quite overshadow my door.
Frivolous, that I am, and so is my patron, Lord Cupid.
    I have the strength of my theme; I have that strength and no
      more.
Venus herself, without me, would seem like a wench from the coun-
      try:
    Aide to that goddess I am, comrade, and go-between.
Doors you cannot unbar, however majestic your presence,
    Open at once with ease, charmed by my flattering words.
I have been able to bear my tribulations with patience,
    Face up to things that would daunt your supercilious eye.
Through me Corinna has learned how to steal away from her watch-
      man,
    How to break down the faith placed in the bolt's barricade,
How to slip from her bed with garments happily loosened,
    How to steal through the night, quiet, sure-footed, and sly.

How many times have the lovers adopted my manner for verses
    Fixed to the cruel doors, ready for any man's eye.
Once, I remember, I hid, tucked away in a maidservant's bodice,
    Lying in wait till the time when the grim watcher was gone.
What about other times, a birthday present, for instance,
    When your barbarous girl gives me no end of ill-use?
I was the first to implant the seeds of your inspiration:
    If she runs after you now, you are indebted to me."
That was enough. I began: "O goddesses both, I implore you,
    Let my timorous words fall on listening ears.
One brings me honor indeed with the lofty buskin and scepter,
    Grave and serious style, solemn and eloquent tone.
One gives fame to my love, enduring honor and blessing:
    Stay at my side for a while; keep the short verse with the long.
Tragedy, grant me delay—a little more time for your poet.
    Yours is an endless toil; what she requires is but brief."
Moved, she granted my prayer: let the tender loves come, let them
      hurry,
    While I have time; at my heels presses a mightier task.

II

I do not sit here because I'm in love with the thoroughbred horses,
    Still, I hope that the one you like will get the job done.
Why have I come? To be talking with you, to be sitting beside you,
    Letting you know, my dear, what you are doing to me.
You watch the races, and I watch you—what a wonderful system!
    Each of us feasting our eyes on the delights that we prize.
The horses are on the track. What's your selection, which rider?
    Lucky, that's what I call him, seeing he's caught your eye.
That should happen to me; I'd give you a run for your money,
    Beating the field from the gate, driving with spurs and with bat,
Cutting across to the rail—still, I might get into trouble,
    In the last eighth or sixteenth, looking for you in the stands,

Maybe let go of the reins, or stand straight up in the stirrups—
    Wasn't it Pelops who fell, scarcely a furlong from home?
No, he came on to win, and that's the way to be winners,
    Hippodameia, you—just so you give us a play.

Why do you edge way off? The spaces are certainly narrow,
    Yes, and a good thing, too, bringing a couple so close.
You on the right, whoever you are, don't jostle the lady,
    That's no way to behave, rubbing against her like that.
You in the row behind, what has become of your manners?
    Pull in your legs, my friend; don't stick your knees in her back.
Look, dear, look at your skirt—isn't it dragging a little?
    Lift it a bit, or—No, I'll take care of it. So.
Hateful old skirt, to be hiding such beautiful knees and such ankles,
    Yes, and the more I look, I figure—hateful old skirt!
Maybe, but this I doubt, she had better legs, Atalanta—
    Milanion, anyway, wanted to lift them aloft.
Such were the limbs of Diana, according to all of the painters,
    When she was girt for the chase, fierce in pursuit of her prey.
Even before I saw, I was burning with violent passion,
    So, add fire to fire, pour water into the sea!
Judging from what I can see, what I can't see must be delightful,
    Hidden though it may be under the silk and the lace.

Stifling? Never mind that. I'll make a fan of my program,
    Or is this heat in the air not from the weather at all,
Not from the weather at all, but the fire in my heart for a woman?
    That speck of dust on your blouse—do let me brush it away.

What's this, a special parade? Time to stand up and be cheering,
    Ivory statues and gold passing in front of our eyes.
Victory first, her wings spread wide. Now hear me, oh goddess,
    Be on my side, I pray; help me to win the day.
Neptune is next, and all very well, if you're fond of the ocean;

Sailors, give him a hand; I like it better on land.
Soldiers, applaud for the War-god; I am a peace-loving fellow,
    Peacetime's better for love; worship Apollo, you bards;
Worship Diana, you hunters; craftsmen, honor Minerva;
    Farmers, give praise to the powers tending the grain and the
        vine;
Boxers, give Pollux acclaim; and troopers cheer for your Castor;
    Here comes the goddess for me, and her boy with the bow at her
        side.
Venus and Cupid, hail! Let me finish what I have started,
    Let my new darling be kind, quickly consenting to love.
Look! Did you see her move? did you see her nod in approval?
    Since she has given the sign, surely you must be mine.
Make good the promise she made, and I will certainly make you
    More of a goddess than she, longer enshrined in my heart.
That can't be any fun, with your legs hanging over and dangling,
    Why don't you stick your toes into the railing in front?

Now the procession is over. The track is clear for the feature;
    Moving up to the gate, *the horses are at the post.*
What are your colors? Red cap, white jacket, red polka dot markings,
    Even the horse seems to know how you expect him to go.
They're off! My God, what a start! what in the world is he doing,
    Look at him, taking him wide, Oh, what a bucketing ride!
Oh, what a stiff we are on, he'll be over the rail in a minute—
    One good thing at this track; the starters can call them back,
Can, and don't think they won't, if the crowd sets up enough booing,
    Boo, boo, boo, boo, boo! So we get a new start.
That's a relief at least. Now, put your head on my shoulder,
    Don't let yourself be upset; I'll tell you when you can look.
Down goes the flag, and they're running, well bunched, that's some-
        thing more like it
    Colors bright in the sun, flashing around the turn,
And here he comes, all by himself, and nothing anywhere near him,

Over the line and the rest whipping and driving behind.
Darling, you had him, you had him. Doesn't that make you feel
    better?
When the right bets are laid, winners are bound to be paid.
But why confine it to bets? She gave me a smile for an answer,
    Nor could I see in her eyes any OBJECTION at all.

III

Go, believe there are gods—she has broken her vows, though she
    swore them,
    Perjuress! yet her good looks suffer no damage, no blast.
She has insulted the gods, but the white and red of her color
    Still shines, rose in the snow; still her dark tresses grow long.
Dainty and narrow her feet; they still are dainty and narrow:
    Tall and comely she was; still she is comely and tall.
She had sparkling eyes; they are still like the stars in the heaven,
    Though she swore by those eyes, swore, and went on to deceive.
Surely the gods are indulgent to girls who break oaths and swear
    falsely:
    Beauty's a privileged caste; all retribution is vain.
Not long ago, I recall, she swore by her eyes, and mine also,
    Swore by her eyes and mine; mine are the ones that feel pain.
Tell me the truth, O gods: if she was the one who deceived you,
    Why do I suffer the grief due to another one's sin?
Well, that is always your way: Andromeda's mother was boastful,
    Arrogant in her good looks; who served the sentence?—the girl.
Isn't it more than enough that to call you to witness means nothing?
    Must her immunity make fools of the gods, and of me?
Must I suffer for her, become her perjury's scapegoat,
    Be her victim and dupe, while the deceitress goes free?
Either God is a word, a name, no more, without substance,
    Frightening silly folk into the vainest belief,
Or, if there is any god he's in love with the girls, and too partial

Letting them do what they please, winking at any offense.
We are the victims of Mars, we men, of his fate-dealing weapons,
     We are the ones at whom Pallas keeps hurling her spear,
We are the target and butt of the bright-flying shafts of Apollo,
     On our heads descend thunderbolts flung from Jove's hand.
Even the reverend gods are afraid of irreverent women:
     When did they ever bring low Beauty's preposterous pride?
Why should any man trouble to come to the altars with incense?
     Where is our spirit, men? what has become of our nerve?
Jupiter hurls his bolts alike at the low and the lofty,
     Partial to no one on earth, only to girls who tell lies.
Many have merited death, but only poor Semele suffered
     All the full power of Jove for her presumptuous love;
Yet, even so, it would seem, he had to atone for it shortly,
     Letting his thigh be the womb out of which Bacchus was born.
What am I crying about? and why am I railing at Heaven?
     Even the gods have hearts, even the gods have eyes.
If I myself were a god, and women, invoking my godhead,
     Swore and forswore themselves, nothing would happen at all.
I'd be the first to swear that women always swore truly;
     I would not let me be called one of the grimmest of gods.
Only one thing, my dear—don't overdo it, go easy,
     Lie if you must, but please!—don't swear false oaths by my eyes.

IV

Setting a guard on your wife? How silly, ridiculous husband!
     She is protected the best whose inclinations are chaste.
Only when license exists does continence hold any value;
     She who keeps pure since she must might just as well be impure.
Granted you prison the body, the mind can break any commandment;
     Stop what she wishes to do, you cannot stop her desire.
Lock up everything else, you can't set a lock on her person;

Isolate everything else, lovers will find a way in.
She who has freedom to sin is apt to be less of a sinner:
     Opportunity says, "When it is easy, who cares?"
Take my advice, don't make temptation more fun by forbidding;
     Victory's easy to win if you're indulgent; give in!
Not long ago I saw a horse, rebellious and fighting,
     Taking the bit in his mouth, flying on wings of the wind,
But as soon as the reins were let loose, and he knew it, he slowed to
          a canter,
     Letting the lines fall free over the wind-tossing mane.
Always our nature insists on things denied and forbidden;
     Always our fever craves water it never should have.
Argus, with all of his eyes, a hundred before and behind him,
     Over and over again nodded, was blinded by Love.
Danae, shut in the tower, the impregnable fortress of iron,
     Went in a maid, but soon welcomed the entrance of Jove.
Never a guard was set on Penelope's comings and goings:
     Suitors might riot and brawl; still her devotion was true.
What we are kept from we want all the more: solicitude always
     Calls to the thief, but few love what another concedes.
It's not her face that attracts, but her husband's excessive devotion;
     There must be something there, men think, to keep you in
          thrall.
She whom her husband guards is not chaste, but desirably wanton;
     Fear makes the price of her charms more than her body deserves.
Whether you like it or not, forbidden pleasure is welcome;
     If she can say, "I'm afraid!" that's the best come-on of all.
Yet it is far from correct to imprison a girl who is freeborn;
     Let that oppression be laid only on those who are slaves.
Is a girl to be pure for the sake of her keeper's credentials,
     So that the watchman can boast "Give all the credit to me!"?
He is a countrified lout, who objects when his wife does some cheat-
          ing,
     Yes, and an ignorant lout, blind to the ways of our town,

74

Founded—or hadn't you heard?—by heroes born out of wedlock,
    Ilia's children, sired, not by a husband, but Mars.
Why take a beautiful wife, if all you want is a pure one?
    Every natural law says you can't have it both ways.
Don't be a fool; let her play; put off that glooming expression;
    Don't be too much of a spouse, always demanding and stiff.
Cherish the things she will bring you—she'll have no enemies,
    really—
    You'll be a popular man, all at a nominal cost,
Dear to the younger set, and in great demand at their parties,
    And you will find in the house gifts that won't cost you a cent!

V

"Night: and my weary eyes were closed in oppressive slumber.
    I had a terrible dream; this was the way it appeared—
At the foot of a sunny hill a forest darkened with holm-oak,
    Hiding many a bird under the gloom of the boughs.
There was a plot of green in the midst, an emerald meadow,
    Moistened by water I heard trickling with delicate sound.
I was avoiding the heat under the shade of the branches,
    Though the heat was there, under the branches' shade.
Suddenly, coming to graze on the grass with its bright-colored flow-
    ers,
    There, before my eyes, stood a white heifer, who shone
Whiter than new-fallen snow before it dissolves into water,
    Whiter than milk in the pail, gleaming with hissing foam,
And there came to her side a bull, her happy companion,
    Both of them folding their knees, sinking to rest on the green.
While he lay there and chewed in his ruminant manner, I noticed
    Slumber relaxed his power; he laid his head on the ground.
Swooping down through the air on noiseless pinions, a raven
    Came and lit on the ground, chattering, clacking away.
Thrice, with a petulant beak, it pecked at the breast of the heifer,

Carried away in its mouth tufts of the snowiest hair.
After a while, so it seemed, the heifer rose and departed,
    Bearing the mark of a bruise dark on the white of her breast,
Saw, far off, other bulls, happily grazing together—
    There were other bulls now, happily grazing the field—
Saw, and hurried her course, and joined these new-found compan-
        ions,
    Browsing on pastures green, rich with luxurious growth.
Tell me, whoever you are, seer of the dreams of the night-time,
    What do my visions mean? what do they bring that is true?"
Thus he spoke in reply, the seer of the dreams of the night-time,
    Weighing with careful mind every detail of my dream:
"The heat that you wanted to shun, and had no luck in the shun-
        ning
    Under the moving leaves, that was the ardor of love.
That white heifer portended your girl, an appropriate color,
    Suitable for your love; the bull, her mate, that was you.
All that pecking her breast by the raven—a nasty old woman
    Tries, like a bawd, to corrupt all the desire of her heart.
The time doesn't matter; the fact that the bull, in the end, was
        deserted
    Proves you will lie alone, cold in a desolate bed.
That black color, the bruise, the spots on the front of the bosom
    Shows the infection, the stain of an adulterous heart."
So the interpreter spoke. My heart felt chill and foreboding
    And the sight of my eyes faced only darkness and night.

VI

River, whose muddy banks are choked by the reeds and the rushes,
    I'm in a hurry toward her—stay your waters a while!
You have no bridge, no ferry to take me across with a cable,
    While I can sit at my ease, ride without pulling an oar.
Once you were small, I remember; I had no terror of crossing;

I could wade all the way, hardly get wet to my shins.
Now you're a torrent in spate, with the snow melting down from the
      mountains,
    Thickened, your waters roll, roily and brown in their flood.
How did it help me at all to have rushed, to have taken from slum-
      ber
    Hours that were proper for rest, adding the night to the day,
If I have to stand here, marking time, and completely resourceless,
    Quite unable to set foot on the opposite shore?
Now I wish that I had those wingèd sandals of Perseus,
    Such as he wore when he flew over the Libyan sands.
Now I wish for the car from which the Earth-mother, Ceres,
    Over the untilled ground scattered the seeds of the corn.
What am I talking about? The lies of the bards are prodigious.
    These are marvels no day ever has seen or will see.
Rather, O river poured over the normal course of your channel,
    Wishing you no bad luck, hadn't you better subside?
Hatred will be your lot, believe me, unbearable hatred,
    Once the word gets around that you halted a poet in love.
Rivers should rush to the aid of lovers, especially young ones;
    Rivers themselves have known all the sensations of love.
Inachus once turned pale at the sight of a girl from Bithynia,
    Melie, that was her name—think how his temperature rose!
Troy had not been under siege for more than a season, when Xan-
      thus,
    River of Troy, fell prey to Neaera's bright eyes.
Did not Alpheus go underground for his lost Arethusa,
    Hunting her far from his home, hunting her under the sea?
I will skip over a few, but let me ask you, Achelous,
    What of your broken horn, shattered by Hercules' hand?
Calydon's worth was less, Aetolia unimportant,
    Deianira alone moved him to such an affray.
That rich river, the seven-mouthed Nile, whose sources are hidden,
    Could not drown with his flood fires that Evanthe inspired.

Trying to dry himself off for Salmoneus' daughter, Enipeus
    Ordered his waves to subside; ordered, they promptly obeyed.
Nor should I leave out the tale of Anio, Tivoli's river,
    Tumbling by hollow rocks, helpful to orchard lands.
Ilia captured his heart, for all her dishevelled appearance,
    Both her cheeks and her hair showing the mark of her nails.
Mourning her uncle's crime, and the rape of the violent War-god,
    Wandering barefoot she went, walking her lonely ways.
Anio, rushing along, looked out from the whirl of his waters,
    Saw her and called aloud in the hoarse voice of his flood:
"Ilia, why are you troubled? Why are you wandering, lonely?
    Where are your fillets of white? Why this neglect of your robes?
Why are your eyes all red with the flood of tears running over?
    Why tear open your dress, beating your breast with your hands?
I would have flint for a heart, or a mechanism of iron,
    If I were not to be moved, seeing the tears in your eyes.
Ilia, put off your fear. My royal palace is open:
    My waves will cherish your grace; Ilia, put off your fear.
You shall be queen of my nymphs, a hundred, or more than hundred;
    Nymphs by the hundred or more dwell in the depths of my stream.
Do not reject me, I pray, Ilia, daughter of Trojans:
    Richer than promise my gifts; look on their giver with love."
So he spoke; but her tears continued to flow, and she stood there,
    Answering never a word, keeping her eyes on the ground.
Thrice she attempted to flee, and thrice she stopped at the margin
    Where the flood ran deep; fear swept her courage away.
Still she tore at her hair, her hands persistent in outrage,
    Spoke, with quivering lips, words called forth by her wrongs:
"Would that my bones had been laid to rest in the tomb of my fathers
    While they were virtuous bones, while I was truly a maid.
I was a Vestal once, a priestess at Ilion's altars,

Now disgraced and defiled—what is a marriage to me?
Why do I live on so, an object of vulgar derision?
    Strumpet, they call me, and worse; death would be better than
       shame."
Desperate, holding her cloak to the eyes all swollen with weeping,
    She threw herself into the stream, and the water bore her away,
But the river, they say, or the god of the river, upheld her,
    Laid his hands on her breast, made her the queen of his bed.
What a long story to prove the passionate nature of rivers!
    Your own lusts, I suppose, woodland and forests conceal.
While I've been talking, it seems, your waters grow deeper and
    wider;
    Out of their channel still rises the full-flowing wave.
Why are you angry at me? Why interfere with my pleasure?
    Churl, oaf, lout, clown, boor, why break the journey begun?
If you were anything much, a river of known reputation,
    If your fame had been spread out to the ends of the world—
But you haven't even a name, you ditch, you rivulet's bastard,
    No respectable source, no fixed channel is yours.
Rain and the melting snows are all you have to sustain you;
    Indolent winter's boon gives you the little you own.
Muddy and brown you run in the opulence of December;
    Yellow and dry you stand, nothing, in August, but sand.
What wayfarer could quench his thirst in that absence, that desert?
    Who, going by, would cry "River, forever flow on!"?
Harmful to herds you run, and even more harmful to pasture:
    This bothers others, perhaps; my own delay bothers me,
So I waste time, like a fool, alluding to amorous rivers,
    Dropping significant names on a poor streamlet like you.
Inachus, Nile, Achelous—all of them owe me a ducking
    In that they come to my mind by this nonentity here.
May you get what you deserve, you muddy, disgusting old nuisance!
    Summer suns scorch you to death, winters forever be dry!

VII

Ugly—is that what she is? Inelegant? Quite unattractive?
    Never, in all my life, object of all my desire?
So, when I had her at last, or at least had the chance to have had her,
    There I lay on the bed, useless, a lummox of lead.
Much as I wanted the girl, and the girl was equally willing,
    I was unable to rise to the occasion at all.
Whiter than mountain snows, her arms moved over my body,
    Tongue was searching for tongue, thigh rubbed up against
        thigh,
Coaxing endearments she spoke, with words never mentioned in
    public,
    Calling me every pet name, calling me lover, and lord.
Still, as if nipped by a frost, my stalk was refusing to burgeon,
    Banner without a staff, all my intention betrayed.
There I lay like a corpse, dead weight, a specimen only,
    Never quite sure in my mind whether a corpse or a ghost.
What will my old age be like, if ever I manage to reach it,
    If in the days of my youth I am no better than this?
I am ashamed of my years—what is it they say?—my young man-
    hood,
    When this girl at my side found me not young, nor a man.
So might a Vestal go forth to offer her pious devotions,
    So might a sister be safe in her dear brother's respect.
Yet, and not long ago, I took Chloe twice, and blonde Pitho
    Three times, and three times satisfied Libas in bed,
But my record was set, if I remember correctly,
    With Corinna—nine times, all in a short summer night.
What is wrong with me now? Has somebody poisoned my members,
    Some one stuck pins in a doll made to resemble my build?
Magical spells, we know, can blight and wither the cornfields,
    Magical spells can dry fountains that leap to the sky.

Acorns can fall from the oaks, and the grapes drop down in the vine-
     yards,
     Apples rot on the bough under enchantment and charm:
Is it impossible, then, to suppose that a spell has unmanned me,
     Striking deep at my root? There'd be some comfort in that.
Added to this was the shame, a secondary infection,
     Making it twice as—No! (I was about to say, *hard*.)
What a girl I saw, and what a girl I was touching!
     She could have done just as well using the fringe of her dress.
The touch of her hand would bring rejuvenation to Nestor;
     Ancient Tithonus would rise, potent for all of his years.
She touched me with her hand, and I responded with nothing.
     What new vows must I make? what new incense prepare?
I can believe the great gods are sorry for what they have offered,
     Knowing their offering vain, put to ignoble ill-use.
I wanted a welcome; I had it: I wanted her kisses; I had them:
     Nothing I did not want; there it was, ready for me.
What was the good of it all? I was rich and yet I was a miser,
     I had a kingdom there, eunuch of all I surveyed.
So might a man die of thirst in a river of bountiful water;
     So might a fruit grower own apples he never could pluck.
Oh, but she tried to help, wasting her kisses upon me,
     Using every technique: all her devices were vain.
She could have moved great oaks, have moved the most resolute
     iron,
     She could have moved deaf stones, coaxing them, teasing them
     so.
She was worthy, be sure, to have roused up any man living:
     I was neither alive, nor was I even a man.
What was the use? None at all—a nightingale singing to deaf-mutes,
     Beautiful works of art on the walls for the blind.
What enjoyment I had, what pleasure in anticipation!
     Nothing was wrong with my mind, bent on inventing new ways,
But my body lay there, of no more use than a dead man's,

Oh what a thing to behold, limper than yesterday's rose!
Look at me now, erect (too late), abounding in vigor,
     Equal to any demand, ready to enter the field.
Why do you act like that, most villainous part of my body?
     You have fooled me before, you and that promise of yours.
You are deluding your master: you let me down, you deceived me,
     Causing me loss and defeat, causing me sorrow and shame.
Yet even so my girl made every effort to rouse you,
     Gently urging you on with the caress of her hand.
When she saw all her arts were wasted, a useless endeavor,
     Your indifference still sullen, unable to rise,
"Why do you mock me?" she cried, "Are you crazy? Or didn't you
          want to?
     Who gave you orders to bring any such slug to my bed?
Either Circe has laid the curse of her magic upon you,
     Or you have come to me tired, worn out by some other girl."
With that, she leaped from the bed, wrapped her loose garments
          around her,
     Rushed, as quick as a wink, barefooted out of the room,
Yet, lest her serving-girls get the idea that no one had touched her
     (Such an unthinkable shame!), made a few spots on the sheet.

VIII

And does any one now look up to the gifts of a writer,
     Any one think that song merits the slightest acclaim?
Genius was worth more, once, than all of the gold of the Indies;
     Now, in this barbarous time, it has no value at all.
When my little books have given my lady some pleasure,
     Where my books could go, I cannot enter, I find.
Once she has given them praise, she shuts her door on the poet;
     Hither and thither I go, my talent, it seems, a disgrace.
Look at what she prefers! A *nouveau riche*, and a killer,
     Come to title and wealth, fat on the slaughter of war.

Can you, my life, put your arms around that kind of a blackguard?
 Can you, my life, be laid in that death-dealer's embrace?
If you don't know, and you should—that head used to carry a hel-
  met;
   That side, which rubs against yours, used to be rubbed by a
    sword.
That left hand, where the new ring shines, once went through a
  shield-strap;
   Touch his right hand: is it still red from an enemy's blood?
How can you touch a hand that you know has been guilty of slaugh-
  ter?
   How can you touch that hand? Where has your tenderness
    gone?
Look at his scars, the marks, the reminders of all of his battles:
   Every possession he has he owes to his body alone.
Ask him how many throats he has cut, and perhaps he will tell you.
   What if he does confess?—You are too greedy to care.
Meanwhile, I, unstained, priest of the Muse and Apollo,
   Sing my song in vain, barred from your obdurate door.
Men who are wiser than I will never follow my calling—
   Better to go to the wars, take up the sword, not the pen.
Jupiter, warning himself that nothing could equal gold's power,
   Turned himself into gold by way of seducing a maid.
While there was nothing to gain, the father was harsh, and the
  maiden
   Strict and severe, the door adamant, iron the tower,
But when his wisdom came down to her in the guise of a profit,
   Gladly she offered herself; what she was bidden, she gave.
Ah, when old Saturn held dominion over the heavens,
   Lucre was something unknown, deep in the dark underground.
Copper and silver and gold were consigned to the shadows of Hades,
   Out of the reach of men, with iron and ore-laden stone,
But he gave better gifts, the natural increase, the harvest
   Out of the untilled ground, the honey found in the oak.

No one furrowed the earth, in those good days, with the plough-
       share,
     No surveyor marked off properties bounded with lines,
No one swept over the seas with oar-blades dipping the waters,
     Mortals knew one frontier—that was the edge of the shore.
Always, O race of man, your wit has been your disaster,
     Cleverness, bent on gain, proved a calamitous loss.
What was the use of surrounding cities with turreted ramparts,
     Arming your hands for war—what in the world was the use?
What was the ocean to you? The land should suffice for content-
       ment.
     Why not covet the sky, greedy for triple domain?
Even now your pretense goes heavenward—temples for Caesar!
     Temples for Ilia's son, Romulus, founder of Rome.
What we raise from the earth, alas! is the harvest of metal;
     Soldiers acquire their wealth out of the reaping of blood.
The Senate is closed to the poor; rank is the pathway to standing;
     Jurors are drawn from the rich; wealth is the warrant of class.
Let them have everything else, lording it over the forum,
     Lording it in the parade, masters in peace and in war,
Just so they leave one thing for a poor man's pride and possession:
     Let them not, in their greed, traffic us out of our loves.
Now, though the girl I adore is as self-controlled as the Sabines,
     He who can give her enough makes her a chattel, a slave.
I am kept from her door by a guard, I menace her husband,
     But if I bring her a gift, husband and guard disappear.
What we need is a god, for lovers, neglected, to pray to,
     A power whose vengeance would turn ill-gotten gain into dust.

IX

Aurora lamenting for Memnon, Thetis in tears for Achilles—
     Even a goddess can mourn sorrowful fates of mankind.
Elegy, loosen your hair: weep for the lot of Tibullus,

Gone to the funeral pyre, singer of your own song.
See how Cupid comes, with the quiver reversed, and the arrows
 Broken, broken the bow, and the light of the torch gone out.
See how he moves, downcast, sobbing with terrible anguish,
 Beating his naked breast, drooping the pitiful wings.
That was the way he seemed, men say, at the rites for Aeneas,
 Leaving Iulus' home, sharing the grief of the son.
Venus sorrowed no less over the death of Tibullus
 Than for Adonis, slain by the fierce tusk of the boar.
Sacred, we poets are called, and the care of the gods in the heaven;
 Sometimes, people have thought, we have within us a god.
Death keeps making demands, profaning everything sacred;
 Death lays darkening hands on all the grace of the world.
Orpheus' song tamed beasts: his mother was one of the Muses;
 He was Apollo's son—talent and lineage vain!
And the same father mourned, deep in the forest, for Linus,
 Crying his name in grief to the unanswering lyre.
Add to these Homer, the source of inspiration forever,
 Gone to the desolate dark, sunk by the drowning of death.
Only the song lives on, the toils at Troy, and the weaving
 Broken at night—be sure these will not suffer the fire.
So may Delia live, and Nemesis, girls of Tibullus,
 One his first love, and one only more recently known.
What was the good of it all, the sacrifice, the devotion,
 Sleeping apart, at times, faithful to Isis alone?
Pardon my telling the truth, but when fate, in its malice, deprives us
 Of our purest and best, then I doubt there are gods.
Live in devotion—you die; observe the rites—in observance
 Death comes heavily down, drags you from temple to tomb.
Trust in beautiful song—even Tibullus is mortal,
 No more left than the ash light in the vault of the urn.
Dedication, it seems, is little defense for a poet;
 Funeral fires were bold even to feed on his heart.
Fires that could do such a thing would prey on the golden temples—

85

Venus averted her gaze, even shed tears at the sight.
Yet it might have been worse, I suppose, had he died in Phaeacia,
    Had that barbarous earth covered a body unsung.
Here, at least, you could have a mother to bring to your ashes
    Sad funereal gifts, closing your eyes at the end,
Here a sister could share the grief of the sorrowing mother,
    Coming with hair unbound, beating her breast with her hand,
Yes, and Nemesis come, and your earlier loved one come with her,
    Both to no lonely pyre, both of them bringing their love,
Delia crying, "At least, I loved you with both of us happy,
    I was a different fire, bringing a life to your heart."
Nemesis making reply, "Mine is the loss you intrude on:
    I was the one toward whom, dying, he reached out his hand."
If we, any of us, are more than a name and a shadow,
    Surely Tibullus will dwell safe in Elysium's vale,
Calvus be there at his side, with ivy binding his temples,
    Calvus, eternally young, Catullus, blessed in his art,
Gallus as well, impulsive at heart, of the generous spirit
    (Surely the charge is a lie, that he was false to his friend).
These will companion your shade, if shade is survivor of body,
    Gentle Tibullus, one more in the abodes of the blest.
Rest in quietude: may the earth weigh light on the ashes,
    May the bones be safe in the embrace of the urn.

X

Autumn: the time of the year for the service in honor of Ceres,
    So my love lies alone, sleeps in a bed unshared.
Goddess of golden hair, with the golden grain at your temples,
    Why must your festival day end our nocturnal delight?
People all over the world hail you as goddess and giver;
    Never was goddess less mean, less stingy of her blessings to men.
Never, until you came, did the shaggy countrymen parch corn,
    Nor was the threshing floor anything, even a name.

Only the ancient oaks, the original oracles, offered
　　Acorns for food, those days; acorns and grass were man's fare.
Ceres was first to teach the seed to swell in the furrow,
　　Ceres was first to reap the red-gold harvest of grain,
Ceres was first to set the yoke on the necks of the oxen,
　　First to penetrate ground, turned by the blade of the plough.
How can anyone think she delights in the weeping of lovers,
　　Think she is truly adored when they lie in their torment alone?
Much as she loves her fields, her fertile acres, believe me
　　She is no rustic maid, love unknown to her heart.
The Cretans can prove my case—the Cretans are not always liars—
　　Crete is the lofty land, proud of the nurture of Jove.
There the god who now controls the heights of the heaven
　　Once was a little child, drinking his milk with the rest.
We can trust their faith, with Jove himself as their witness,
　　Even Ceres, I think, surely would own it was true,
True that under Mount Ida she looked on Iasius hunting,
　　Watched his unfaltering hand piercing the wild beast's side,
Watched him, and felt the fire of passion feed on her marrow,
　　Drawn this way and that, love contending with shame.
Shame was the victim of love: the fields and the furrows grew arid,
　　All the seed that was sown yielded but scanty return.
Though the pick was aimed well to break the clods, and the plough-
　　　　share
　　Drove through the stubborn ground, though the seed was well-
　　　　sown,
All was in vain: the toil of the year a wanton delusion,
　　Husbandmen found their vows made to no purpose at all.
Deep in the woods she lurked, the potent goddess of increase,
　　Fallen from her gold hair lay the dry chaplets of grain.
Only in Crete was the harvest rich in its yield, and abundant,
　　Where the goddess had gone, there there was plenty, alone.
Ida, dark home of the woods, was white with the hoarfrost of har-
　　　　vest;

Wheat, in the forest groves, fell to the tusk of the boar.
Minos, giver of law, prayed for such seasons forever,
    Prayed that Ceres' love so might forever endure.
Golden goddess, for whom the lying alone was a sorrow,
    Why must I suffer so, now on your holy day?
Why must I be sad, when you have discovered your daughter
    Queen of a world whose pride yields to Juno's alone?
Holidays call for love and wine and singing and dancing—
    Those are the comeliest gifts for us to bring to our gods.

XI A

My patience ends: I have endured too long.
Begone, base love, from my exhausted breast.
Free now, I flee the fetters of my wrong,
Shamed by my lack of shame, at last confessed.
I win. I spurn the love that conquered me,
Put laurels on my brow (and late enough!).
Ovid, persist, endure: the draught may be
Bitter to taste, but it is healing stuff.

How did I ever stand it—from your door
Banished, a freeborn man, to lie all night
On the hard ground? A slave could do no more,
Guarding your portals, barriers kept tight,
Till out he came, this nobody, your love,
So spent, so weak, that he could hardly move.

Disgusting so to see him, but the shame
Would be the greater had he seen me there.
Did I not always cherish your good name,
Guard you with love, escort you everywhere?
People were fond of you, and well you know it,
Because I loved you—what a thing to do,

Telling those monstrous falsehoods to your poet,
Swearing to me that you were always true!

You'd wink and nod at rivals; you would be
Unwell, or so you said; I'd come and find
You'd made a marvelous recovery,
Unkind to me, to others more than kind.
Get someone else to take all this, because
I am no longer the damn fool I was.

XI B

I fight against my fickle heart, that goes
This way and that, toward love, or else toward hate.
I'll hate, if possible, but I suppose
That love will win, as usual; my fate,
More than my will, puts me at love's command.
Oxen love not the yoke, but they submit.
I flee your worthlessness, you understand,
But love your beauty, and am drawn to it.

Behavior such as yours I must despise;
A body such as yours I must adore.
My heart, I know, is prompting me with lies,
My mind is useless, as it was before.
So, though I never trust and always doubt you,
I cannot manage with you or without you.

Your beauty should be less, or else your ways
More decent; your behavior merits scorn,
And yet your charm appeals for love and praise,
Alas for me, that I was ever born,
Who have to make decision, when the crime
Is venial if the criminal resorts

To oaths once sworn in bed—O happier time!—
With gods conspiring to corrupt the courts.

So, by your beauty, which, I must confess,
Is not without divinity, swear me true,
But whether you say me No, or say me Yes,
The only question in my loving you
Is, shall it be with, or against, your will?
For never a doubt that I shall love you still.

XII

What day was that, you birds not white, when you chanted the
        omens
    Boding portentous grief to a poet always in love?
What kind of star must I think is rising in opposition?
    In my complaints of the gods, which are the movers of war?
She who was recently mine, and, in the beginning, mine only,
    Now, I'm afraid, I must share with an inordinate host.
Can I be wrong to suppose that she owes her fame to my verses?
    I have no doubt that my art makes her the talk of the town.
So much the worse for me! Why did I herald her beauty?
    Herald?—No, auctioneer! She is a creature for sale.
I am her pander, her pimp, I serve as guide for her lovers,
    Mine is the hand that turns, slyly, her opening door.
Whether there's profit in verse, I doubt very much: mine has always
    Brought me damage and hurt, stood in the way of my good.
I could have written of Thebes, of Troy, of the exploits of Caesar;
    Only Corinna inspired adequate themes for my art.
Would that the Muses had turned their backs when I started com-
        posing,
    Would that Apollo had frowned even before I began!
People, of course, are inclined to pay no attention to poets;
    I made it worse for myself, wanting my verse to be light.

Yet—our lines made known the treason of Scylla, the forelock
  Torn from the brow of her sire, the ravening dogs at her groin.
We have put wings on feet, have mingled tresses with serpents,
  We have made Pegasus rise, borne on the rush of his wings,
We stretched Tityos out, nine acres for vultures to feed on,
  We gave the triple-mouthed dog the collar of snakes on his
    neck,
We made Enceladus, the thousand-armed javelin-hurler,
  We sang the Sirens' song, fatal temptation to men.
We were the ones who shut the winds in the sack of Ulysses,
  We made Tantalus thirst, up to his neck in the stream,
We made Niobe rock, we made a bear of Callisto,
  We made the nightingale cry, always, her dolorous song.
Jupiter, changing himself to a bird, to a bull, to a downpour
  All bright golden rain, testifies what we can do.
What is the need of recalling the dragon's teeth, or the great bulls
  Breathing fire and flame, or the mutable god from the sea,
Or Phaethon's sisters, whose tears, as they mourned him, changed
    into amber,
  Or the vessels from Troy, Nereids under the wave?
Why should we tell of the day dark over Atreus' tables,
  Tell of the walls that rose, lifted to sounds of the lyre?
There are no limits at all to the fertile license of poets;
  On our unscrupulous art history cannot rely.
So—when I praised a girl, you might have suspected some lying:
  Gullible fools that you are, you'll be the ruin of me.

XIII

Because my wife came from this orchard town
Beyond the walls Camillus once laid low,
We made our journey hither, up and down,
By the steep roads where men must travel slow,
But worth the trouble, for the festival

Of Juno was in preparation there,
With solemn games, and sacrifice, and all
The priestesses in waiting, chaste and fair.

There is an ancient clearing, dark with shade,
Where no one could deny a presence dwells,
Whose altar, very old and rudely made,
Receives the gifts which faithfulness compels,
Incense and prayer, as the procession moves,
Called by flute-music, to the holy groves.

Over the carpet of the forest floor
They wend their way, the heifers, snowy-white,
Faliscan-bred, from the green meadow-shore,
With little calves, not yet a fearful sight,
Although they seem to think so, and the big
Lord of the flock, the ram, whose yellow eye
Is shadowed by his curving horns, the pig,
A humbler victim from the lowly sty.

But no she-goats are there, for people say
That Juno hates the she-goat, who, it seems,
Was once a tattletale, blatting away
Some forest secret, one of Juno's schemes,
So even now the children's sticks and stones
May rattle off the wicked creature's bones.

Before the goddess comes, young men and maids
Prepare the way, sweeping her avenues
With trailing robes, and on their lovely heads
Are gold and jewels, and their little shoes
Are all of gold, and on their heads they bear
Those ancient sacred offerings of hers,

And all the crowd is silent. She is there,
Attended by her golden ministers.

From Argos came this ceremonial:
When Agamemnon fell, Halaesus came,
Leaving his father's wealth, to found this wall
With happier auspice, though with lesser name.
O friendly folk, may Juno's ritual shine
Forever honored, in your eyes and mine!

XIV

Since you are lovely, I know, of course, I can't stop you from cheat-
    ing;
    All that I hope for, at best, is not to know when you do.
I am no censor to say that you always have to be decent:
    Still, I wish you would try, or at least pretend that you are.
She who denies her guilt is never utterly guilty—
    Only the guilt confessed brings the disgrace to her name.
What kind of madness is this, to broadcast most intimate secrets,
    Letting the light of day flood the events of the night?
Even the commonest tart receives her lovers with caution,
    Keeping the people away, sliding the bolt on the door.
You, on the other hand, delight in the role of informer;
    Scandal that implicates you, you are the first to make known.
Have better sense, or, at least, pretend to be one of the modest;
    Let me think you behave, no matter what you may do.
Fay ce que vouldras: only deny that you do so;
    Don't be ashamed to speak properly once in a while.
Everything in its place—and once you get in the bedroom
    Fill it with every delight: let's have no modesty there.
Once you are out of there, though, abandon abandonment, dar-
    ling—
    Bed is the only place where you can act as you please.

There it is no disgrace to fling your dress in a corner,
      There it is no disgrace lying with thigh under thigh,
There it is proper for tongue, as well as for lips, to be kissing,
      There let passion employ all the inventions of love.
There use all of the words, the helpful cries, and the whispers;
      There let the squeak of the bed seem to be keeping in time.
But, when you put on your dress, put on a decent appearance;
      Try not to look like a girl who has been recently—loved.
Lie to the people, to me; fool me, but don't let me know it;
      Let my folly enjoy all of its ignorant bliss.
Why must I see, all the time, the love-notes coming and going?
      Why must I see, in the bed, signs it was slept in by two?
Why must I see your hair disordered, not simply by slumber?
      Why must I see, on your neck, marks of another man's bite?
What are you trying to do, make me see you, *flagrante delicto?*
      Spare me that much, at least, though you don't spare your good
         name.
I am out of my senses, I die, when you boast of promiscuous con-
         duct;
      Through my veins the blood runs with the frigidest chill.
Then I love, then I hate—in vain, for I cannot help loving.
      Then I would gladly be dead, wishing you dead at my side.
I'll not go snooping around, I'll not pursue you with questions;
      If you prefer to keep still, I'll let the sleeping dog lie.
If you are caught in the act, deny it, deny it, deny it!
      You will convince me, of course. "I can't believe my own eyes!"
I am an easy prey, because I want to be conquered.
      All you need is a tongue, saying three words, "I did not!"
That's all you need, no more—you might lose your case in a court-
         room,
      Not so in chambers where I act as both jury and judge!

XV

Seek a new poet, mother of the loves!
My elegies now have their goal in sight.
What I have done, Sulmo, I hope, approves,
Sharing with me this honor, this delight.
I come, if that means anything at all,
From a long lineage, of Paelignian race,
A tribe that sprang to arms at freedom's call
When Rome was fearful of her lofty place.

I am no upstart lord, with title won
In recent wars: if Mantua takes pride
In Virgil's art, or if Verona's son,
Catullus, merits praise that will abide,
So may I, Ovid, win Paelignian glory
And be recalled in Sulmo's song and story.

A little town it is, with water blessed,
Whose walls defend no great domain of ground,
Where, it may chance, some traveller may rest,
Some tourist take his time to look around,
Reminded that a poet came from here,
And say, "O little town, O small estate,
However unimportant you appear,
Because of him I call you truly great."

Venus and Cupid, reverenced with love,
Remove your golden emblems from my field!
With mightier steeds on mightier course I move:
A graver wand has struck me; I must yield.
Congenial Muse, unwarlike Elegy,
Farewell—and may my work live after me!

THE ART
OF
BEAUTY

Listen and learn, dear girls, how to improve your appearance,
    By what methods to keep beauties you want to preserve.
Culture's the word—thereby the briers die out in the farm lands,
    Culture produces the grain out of the bountiful soil,
Culture improves the taste, if the flavor of apples is bitter;
    From the graft of the tree opulent richness is born.
Culture's a pleasant thing: the halls of a palace are gilded;
    Marble with dazzling white covers the blackness of earth;
Fleeces are often dyed with the color of Tyrian crimson;
    Indian ivory carved into the bright figurines.
Maybe, in ancient days, the Sabine daughters of Tatius
    Thought more of tending their fields, thought less of tending
        themselves,
When the mother, red-faced, and perched on a stool or a high-chair,
    Kept the work going along, spinning with calloused thumb,
Folded the lambs and the ewes her daughters had driven to pasture,
    Split up the kindling, and lugged heavier logs for the fire.
Daughters, in our own day, are frail and delicate creatures,
    Fonder of brighter array, garments embroidered with gold,
Hair perfumed, and set in every conceivable fashion,
    Rings on their fingers, and wrists dangling with bracelets and
        charms,

Necklaces brought from the east, and earrings heavy with jewels—
    Double their weight, and one ear hardly could carry the load.
Nothing is wrong with all this, dear girls, if you're trying to please
    us:
    Even the men in our time cultivate elegant style.
Husbands have learned from their wives, and gained no little in
    polish;
    Where is the bride who brings no dower of *chic* to her groom?
Surely it matters—of course!—for whom you are being attractive,
    Who is the love you pursue. Be smart: you'll never go wrong.
Bury yourself on a farm, but, even so, keep your hair neat:
    Hide in the hills; the hills are swarming with elegant girls.
No matter who you may be, to please yourself is a pleasure;
    Dear to the heart of a girl is her own beauty and charm.
Why not? Juno's bird spreads out her feathers to please us,
    Nor is the peacock alone vain of its color and form.
This is a better approach than the use of magic and potions,
    Simples and herbs that a witch gathers with terrible hand.
Put not your trust in herbs, nor distillations, nor juices,
    Oestrogens, wild mares' bane, any intoxicant brews.
Snakes are not split in two by the incantations of Marsians,
    Nor does the wave return backward because of their spells.
Rattle the copper and bronze, and bang away on the cymbals—
    This will not shake the moon out of her heavenly car.

Look, girls: one thing first—you have to think of your conduct.
    When the character's right, looks are a greater delight.
There is a love that will last: age will lay waste to your beauty,
    Time, with remorseless plough, wrinkle and furrow the brow.
There will come a day when you hate to look into a mirror,
    When your grief and your pain double the wrinkles again.
Goodness is more than enough, and time can never outwear it;
    Long as your days will run, love rests securely thereon.

Now learn how, when your limbs begin to stir from their slumber,
  Faces can shine and be bright, fresh as the new-risen sun.
Take the barley that comes from Libya, over the water,
  Strip it of chaff and husks; see that it comes to ten pounds.
Take an equal amount of vetch, and mix them together,
  Soak the mixture in eggs, half an egg to the pound—
After it dries in the wind, have it ground fine by the millstone,
  With it grind up as well antlers a stag has shed.
Add two ounces of this, mix with the grain, and then sift it,
  Add twelve daffodil bulbs after removing the skins
(Pound them on marble first), then a pound and a half of pure
    honey,
  Gum and Tuscan seed weighing a sixth of a pound.
Then apply, and observe—if you've followed directions precisely—
  How your complexion will shine, polished and smooth as your
    glass.

Here is another prescription: roast the white seeds of the lupine,
  Fry, at the same time, beans; let there be six pounds of each.
Grind them up in a mill, and add white lead, the foam of red nitre,
  Also the iris that comes out of Illyrian soil.
Get some strong young man to reduce the mixture to powder,
  So that it weighs, in the end, only one-twelfth of a pound.
Acne can quickly be cured by a dose from the nests of the sea birds
  (They will complain, of course); this is called Halcyon-cream.
Very little is needed, half an ounce; mix it with honey,
  That golden Attican kind, making an unguent or paste.

Incense has other uses besides being burned on the altars;
  Do not use all of your store in the appeasing of gods.
Nitre eliminates warts; put incense and nitre together,
  Just four ounces of each; add three-fourths of a pound
Of gum that's been stripped of its bark, then add a small cube of
    myrrh to it:

Pound it all well, then sift, using honey as base.
Also, it's useful to add fennel to sweet-smelling myrtle,
    A fifth of an ounce to a third—that would be just about right.
Add some dried rose-leaves, let's say a generous handful,
    Also some frankincense, and a sprinkle of Libyan salt.
Over this mixture pour sufficient syrup of barley:
    Let the rose-leaves and salt equal the incense in weight.
When this is smeared on your face, it is very swift and effective:
    Only a moment or so—all your complexion will glow.
I knew a girl, one time, whose lotion consisted of poppies
    Crushed and soaked for a while in ice-water——

(THE POEM SEEMS TO BREAK OFF, RATHER THAN END: EDITORS SUSPECT
GAPS IN THE TEXT, AND CONSIDER THE POEM, IN THE VERSION WE HAVE,
AN UNFINISHED PRODUCTION.)

THE ART
OF LOVE

BOOK

I

This is a book for the man who needs instruction in loving.
  Let him read it and love, taught by the lines he has read.
Art is a thing one must learn, for the sailing, or rowing, of vessels,
  Also for driving a car: love must be guided by art.
Automedon excelled with the reins in the car of Achilles,
  Tiphys in Jason's craft, crafty with rudder and sail;
Thanks be to Venus, I too deserve the title of master,
  Master of Arts, I might say, versed in the precepts of love.
Love, to be sure, is wild and often inclined to resent me;
  Still, he is only a boy, tender and easily swayed.
When Achilles was young, Chiron could tame his wild spirit,
  Even could teach his hands how to move over a lyre.
He, who frightened his foes, and frightened his friends just as often,
  Dreaded one agèd man, so all the ages believe.
He would reach out his hands, submissive and meek, for a lashing:
  Those were the violent hands Hector was later to know.
Chiron instructed Achilles, and I am Cupid's preceptor,
  Each of them savage and rough, each one a goddess's son.
Yet, in good time, as bulls accept the yoke and the ploughshare,
  As the wild horses submit, taking the bridle and bit,
So will Love yield to me, though he wounds my heart with his ar-
  rows,

Whirls his torch in the air, showering sparks from the brand.
So much the worse for him: the more he pierces and burns me,
   I shall avenge all the more all of the wounds he has made.
I am no liar to claim that my art has come from Apollo,
   Nor am I taught my song by the voices of birds in the air,
Neither has Clio appeared at my side, with all of her sisters,
   While I was tending my flocks out in some countryside vale.
No: I have learned what I know from experience, take my word for
      it.
   It is the truth you will hear. Venus, give aid to my song!
Keep far away, stern looks and all of modesty's emblems,
   Headdresses worn by the pure, skirts hiding feet in their folds.
What is the theme of my song? A little pleasant indulgence.
   What is the theme of my song? Nothing that's very far wrong.

First, my raw recruit, my inexperienced soldier,
   Take some trouble to find the girl whom you really can love.
Next, when you see what you like your problem will be how to win
      her.
   Finally, strive to make sure mutual love will endure.
That's as far as I go, the territory I cover,
   Those are the limits I set: take them or leave them alone.

While you are footloose and free to play the field at your pleasure,
   Watch for the one you can tell, "I want no other but you!"
She is not going to come to you floating down from the heavens:
   For the right kind of a girl you must keep using your eyes.
Hunters know where to spread their nets for the stag in his covert,
   Hunters know where the boar gnashes his teeth in the glade.
Fowlers know brier and bush, and fishermen study the waters
   Baiting the hook for the cast just where the fish may be found.
So you too, in your hunt for material worthy of loving,
   First will have to find out where the game usually goes.
I will not tell you to sail searching far over the oceans,

I will not tell you to plod any long wearisome road.
Perseus went far to find his dusky Indian maiden;
    That was a Grecian girl Paris took over the sea.
Rome has all you will need, so many beautiful lovelies
    You will be bound to say, "Here is the grace of the world!"
Gargara's richness of field, Methymna's abundance of vineyard,
    All the fish of the sea, all the birds in the leaves,
All the stars in the sky, are less than the girls Rome can offer;
    Venus is mother and queen here in the town of her son.
If you are fond of them young, you will find them here by the thousands,
    Maids in their teens, from whom you will have trouble to choose.
Maybe a bit more mature, a little bit wiser? Believe me,
    These will outnumber the first as they come trooping along.

Take your time, walk slow, when the sun approaches the lion.
    There are porticoes, marbled under the shade,
Pompey's, Octavia's, or the one in Livia's honor,
    Or the Danaids' own, tall on the Palatine hill.
Don't pass by the shrine of Adonis, sorrow to Venus,
    Where, on the Sabbath day, Syrians worship, and Jews.
Try the Memphian fane of the Heifer, shrouded in linen;
    Isis makes many a girl willing as Io for Jove.
Even the courts of the law, the bustle and noise of the forum,
    (This may be hard to believe) listen to whispers of love.
Hard by the marble shrine of Venus, the Appian fountain,
    Where the water springs high in its rush to the air,
There, and more than once, your counsellor meets with his betters,
    All his forensic arts proving of little avail;
Others he might defend; himself he cannot; words fail him,
    Making objections in vain; Cupid says, *Overruled!*
Venus, whose temple is near, laughs at the mortified creature,
    Lawyer a moment ago, in need of a counsellor now.

Also, the theater's curve is a very good place for your hunting,
    More opportunity here, maybe, than anywhere else.
Here you may find one to love, or possibly only have fun with,
    Someone to take for a night, someone to have and to hold.
Just as a column of ants keeps going and coming forever,
    Bearing their burdens of grain, just as the flight of the bees
Over the meadows and over the fields of the thyme and the clover,
    So do the women come, thronging the festival games,
Elegant, smart, and so many my sense of judgment is troubled.
    Hither they come, to see; hither they come, to be seen.
This is a place for the chase, not the chaste, and Romulus knew it,
    Started it all, in fact; think of the Sabine girls.
There were no awnings, then, over the benches of marble,
    There were no crimson flowers staining the platform's floor,
Only the natural shade from the Palatine trees, and the stage-set
    Quite unadorned, and the folk sitting on steps of sod,
Shading their foreheads with leaves, studying, watching intently,
    Each for the girl he would have, none of them saying a word.
Then, while the Tuscan flute was sounding its primitive measure,
    While the dancer's foot thrice beat the primitive ground,
While the people roared in uninhibited cheering,
    Romulus gave the sign. They had been waiting. They knew.
Up they leaped, and their noise was proof of their vigorous spirit.
    Never a virgin there was free from the lust of a hand.
Just as the timid doves fly from the swooping of eagles,
    Just as the newest lamb tries to escape from the wolf,
So those girls, fearing men, went rushing in every direction;
    Every complexion, through fright, turning a different hue.
Though their fear was the same, it took on different guises:
    Some of them tore their hair; some of them sat stricken dumb.
One is silent in grief, another calls for her mother,
    One shrieks out, one is still; one runs away, and one stays.
So, they are all carried off, these girls, the booty of husbands,
    While, in many, their fear added endowments of charm.

If one struggled too much, or refused to go with her captor,
    He'd pick her up from the ground, lift her aloft in his arms,
Saying, "Why do you spoil your beautiful eyes with that crying?
    Wasn't your mother a wife? That's all I want you to be."
Romulus, you knew the way to give rewards to your soldiers!
    Give me rewards such as these, I would enlist for the wars.
So, to this very day, the theater keeps its tradition:
    Danger is lurking there still, waiting for beautiful girls.

Furthermore, don't overlook the meetings when horses are running;
    In the crowds at the track opportunity waits.
There is no need for a code of finger-signals or nodding.
    Sit as close as you like; no one will stop you at all.
In fact, you will have to sit close—that's one of the rules, at a race track.
    Whether she likes it or not, contact is part of the game.
Try to find something in common, to open the conversation;
    Don't care too much what you say, just so that every one hears.
Ask her, "Whose colors are those?"—that's good for an opening gambit.
    Put your own bet down, fast, on whatever she plays.
Then, when the gods come along in procession, ivory, golden,
    Outcheer every young man, shouting for Venus, the queen.
Often it happens that dust may fall on the blouse of the lady.
    If such dust should fall, carefully brush it away.
Even if there's no dust, brush off whatever there isn't.
    Any excuse will do: why do you think you have hands?
If her cloak hangs low, and the ground is getting it dirty,
    Gather it up with care, lift it a little, so!
Maybe, by way of reward, and not without her indulgence,
    You'll be able to see ankle or possibly knee.
Then look around and glare at the fellow who's sitting behind you,
    Don't let him crowd his knees into her delicate spine.
Girls, as everyone knows, adore these little attentions:

Getting the cushion just right, that's in itself quite an art;
Yes, and it takes a technique in making a fan of your program
Or in fixing a stool under the feet of a girl.
Such is the chance of approach the race track can offer a lover.
There is another good ground, the gladiatorial shows.
On that sorrowful sand Cupid has often contested,
And the watcher of wounds often has had it himself.
While he is talking, or touching a hand, or studying entries,
Asking which one is ahead after his bet has been laid,
Wounded himself, he groans to feel the shaft of the arrow;
He is a victim himself, no more spectator, but show.

Caesar is ready now to add to the world he has conquered:
Our dominion extends; soon the far East will be ours,
Crassus will be avenged, and the Parthians pay for their murders,
No barbarian pride lower our banners again.
Now an avenger is here, in the early prime of his manhood,
A captain ripe for the wars, hardly more than a boy.
Cease, O timid souls, to judge the gods by their birthdays!
When a Caesar is born, valor anticipates time.
Heavenly genius matures more quickly than years in their passing,
Looks, with imperious scorn, on the slow tides of delay.
Hercules, only a child when he strangled the snakes in his cradle,
Proved to be more than a child, worthy descendant of Jove.
Bacchus, who still is a youth, was hardly more than a baby
When the Indian tribes dreaded his conquering wands.
Here is a youth for the wars, with the luck and nerve of his father,
He will be victor indeed, thanks to that luck and that nerve.
Victory must be his due, the name he bears being mighty,
Prince of the young men now, prince of the elders some day.
Since he has brothers, he must avenge the wrongs of his brothers,
Since his father is great, he must defend that renown.
Father and fatherland both summon and arm him for battle;
Enemy hands would grasp realms that belong to his sire.

His are the righteous arms, and the foe bears dastardly weapons;
     Justice and duty will stand where his banners are flown.
Lost in their cause, let the foe be also losers in battle,
     Let our captain bring spoils from the Orient to Rome.
Father Mars, father Caesar, bestow your grace on his going:
     One of you is a god; some day the other will be.
If I'm a prophet at all, you will win, and my anthems will praise you;
     Loud shall be my song, uttering paeans of praise.
Halting to cheer your troops, you will use my words to address
          them—
     May no words of mine fail the great heart in your breast.
Parthians I shall sing, in flight as the Romans press onward,
     I shall sing of the darts flung in their cowardly flight.
If you flee to win, what will you do when you're losing,
     Parthian? Even now yours is an ill-omened name.
So there will come a day when our young Caesar will triumph,
     Handsome and all in gold, drawn by his four snow-white steeds.
Chieftains will lead the way, with chains on their necks and their
          shoulders,
     Such a burden of chains they cannot flee as before.
Happy young men, with happy young girls at their sides, will be
          watching,
     All of their hearts, that day, overflowing with joy.
One of the girls may ask about the names of the monarchs,
     Borne in triumphal array, mountains, or places, or streams.
Answer her questions, each one, and don't always wait till she asks
          you;
     Things that you may not know tell her as if you were sure.
"Why, that's Euphrates, of course, with the reeds hanging over his
          forehead;
     The one with the dark-blue hair? That would be Tigris, his
          twin.
Those are Armenians there; the one just passing is Persia—
     What was that just went by? Some Achaemenian town."

This one, or that, is a leader—call them by name, or by title.
    Get the names right if you can; anyway, have them ring true.

Parties are also fine, not only for food on the tables.
    Something more than the wine you will find there if you look.
Often Bacchus lies there at his ease, and bright-colored Cupid,
    Soft-armed Cupid, near by, coaxes with wheedling charm,
Finds that his thirsty wings are suddenly sprinkled with wine-drops,
    Stands in his place, weighed down, almost unable to move,
Shakes out his dripping plumes, to be sure, in all kinds of a hurry—
    This may hurt more than you think, getting a dousing from love.
Wine sets the spirit afire, and wine brings passionate ardor;
    When there is plenty of wine, sorrow and worry take wing,
Then the laughter comes, and even the poor man has plenty,
    Wrinkles and frowns depart, grief is gone from the heart,
Then simplicity comes, and the inhibitions are banished,
    Slyness dispelled by a grace all too rare in our day.
That is the time when the girls can capture the hearts of their young
    men:
    When you have Venus in wine, then you have fire in fire.
Don't, at any such time, put too much faith in the lamplight.
    Judgment of beauty can err, what with the wine and the dark.
In the full light of the day the judgment of Paris was given;
    That was the time when he said, "Venus, no doubt that you
    win."
Flaws are hidden at night, and every flaw is forgiven;
    When the cats are all gray, then are the women all fair.
Take the advice of the light when you're looking at linens or jewels;
    Looking at faces or forms, take the advice of the day.

Why should I mention them all, the gathering-places of women?
    They are as many—no, more than all the sands of the shore,
Baiae, for instance, or Bath (as the British barbarians call it),
    Where the waters steam sulphurous out of the ground.

I can remember a man who said, "Those waters are deadly!"
    Not without reason, it seems; he had a wound in his heart.
Not so far out of town is the temple of woodland Diana,
    Where the assassin and priest carries the sword in his hand.
She is a virgin: she hates the flying arrows of Cupid;
    Many a wound she has caused; many a wound she will give.

What you've been reading, thus far, has instructed you where to go
    hunting.
    Now you must learn (this is hard) how you can capture your
    find.
Men, whoever you are, and wherever, pay careful attention.
    You common folk, stand by; favor my promises now.

First: be a confident soul, and spread your nets with assurance.
    Women can always be caught; that's the first rule of the game.
Sooner would birds in the spring be silent, or locusts in August,
    Sooner would hounds run away when the fierce rabbits pursue,
Than would a woman, well-wooed, refuse to succumb to a lover;
    She'll make you think she means No! while she is planning her
    Yes!
Love on the sly delights men; it is equally pleasing to women.
    Men are poor at pretense; women can hide their desire.
It's a convention, no more, that men play the part of pursuer.
    Women don't run after us; mousetraps don't run after mice.
In the soft meadows the heifer lows for the bull to come to her,
    Stallions respond, but the mare gives the first whinnying call.
Masculine passion, it seems, is not so wildly abandoned:
    We know its right true end; we can tell when we should stop.
Think of Byblis, who yearned to go to bed with her brother,
    Guilty, yet brave to atone, hanging herself from a beam.
Then there was Myrrha, who loved her father, but not as a daughter,
    Myrrha, a prisoner now, held by the bark of a tree
Whence her tears distil, and we use their fragrance for ointment,

And the drops from the tree are called by her name, the myrrh.
Once in the shadowy vales, the wooded uplands of Ida,
    Roamed a snow-white bull, glory and pride of the herd.
There was one black spot between the horns of his forehead,
    That was his only mark, all of the rest white as milk.
All the heifers of Cnossus, and all the Cydonean heifers
    Wanted him riding their backs—that was their prayer and de-
    sire.
Pasiphae, the queen, desired this bull for her lover,
    Jealous, with hate in her heart for all the beautiful cows.
I sing of things well-known, and Crete can never deny them,
    Liar though Crete may be through all her hundreds of towns.
Pasiphae, I say, with hands not used to such labors,
    Gathered new leaves and young grass, holding them out to the
    beast,
Went where the heifers would go, and had no thought of her hus-
    band,
    Minos, the lord of Crete. (He, too, was horned, it appears.)
Ah, what good did it do to put on her costliest dresses?
    To such a lover as hers riches meant nothing at all.
Why take a mirror along, seeking the herds on the mountains?
    Why, in your foolishness, constantly tend to your hair?
Still, the mirror is right in telling you that you're no heifer,
    Nor, however you wish, can you grow horns on your brow.
Does not Minos suffice? Why seek an adulterous lover?
    If he must be deceived, then let it be with a man.
Leaving her bower, the queen goes to the glades and the woodlands,
    As the Bacchanals go when the Aonian calls.
Often she looked at a cow, and frowned with a jealous expression,
    "How in the world," she says, "can he find pleasure in her?
Look how she lumbers and leaps before him over the meadows,
    Nor do I doubt the damn fool thinks she's a beautiful sight."
Then she would order the beast, poor thing, to be led from the
    pasture,

Put the yoke on her neck, set her to hauling the plough,
Or, on some pretense of sacrificial devotion,
   Have her struck down, and hold entrails in jubilant hands,
Pleasing the altars of gods with the slaughtered corpse of a rival,
   "Go now, and please our lord!" her benediction would be.
Sometimes she wished she had been Io, and sometimes Europa;
   One was a cow for a while, one carried off by a bull.
Finally had her way, devising a heifer of maple,
   So her Minotaur son proved the success of the sire.
Had Aerope abstained from her guilty love of Thyestes
   (Pleasing one man alone seems such a lesson to learn!)—
Never would Phoebus have turned his car from the town of
      Mycenae,
   Wheeling his steeds around, reining them back to the East.
Scylla, the daughter of Nisus, stole from the head of her father
   That one precious lock: now the hounds rage in her womb.
Agamemnon survived the wars and the violent oceans,
   Victim in his own halls, slain by a murderous wife.
Who has not mourned for the flames of Ephyrean Creusa
   Or the mother's hands, stained with the blood of her sons?
Phoenix, the son of Amyntor, weeping from eyes that were blinded,
   Theseus' dismembered son, torn by his horses in fright,
Phineus, blinding his sons, the victims of false accusation,
   Suffering in his turn torments of hunger and doom—
All of these crimes, every one, arose from the lust of a woman,
   Keener in their desire, fiercer, more wanton than ours.
So, you need have little doubt when it comes to winning them over;
   Out of the many there are, hardly a one will refuse.
If they say Yes, or say No, they're pleased with the invitation:
   Even suppose you guess wrong, it costs you nothing to try.
But why should you be wrong? Untried delights are a pleasure:
   Those which we do not own tempt with attraction and charm.
In the fields of our neighbor the grass forever is greener;
   Always the other man's herd offers the richer reward.

Take some trouble, at first, to make her handmaiden's acquaintance:
    She, more than any one else, really can lighten your way.
She must be one you can trust, if she knows of the tricks you are
        playing,
    Confidante, wise and discreet, high in her mistress' regard.
Spoil her by promising much, and spoil her by pleading a little,
    What you seek you will find, if she is willing you should.
She will choose the right time—a maid is as good as a doctor—
    When she is in the right mood, all the more ripe to be had.
When she is in the right mood, you will know it because she is
        happy,
    Like the flowers in the field, seeming to burst into bloom.
When the hearts are glad, and sorrow does not confine them,
    Then they are open wide, and Venus steals coaxingly in.
Troy, in her days of gloom, was well defended by armor;
    When she rejoiced, the horse entered with Greeks in its womb.
It is worth making a try when she's grieving because of a rival,
    Vengeance can quickly be hers if you're conveniently there.
While her maid is at work, combing her hair in the morning,
    Let her keep urging her on, let her add oars to the sail,
Let her say with a sigh, or the softest murmuring whisper,
    "I don't suppose, after all, there is a thing you can do,"
Then let her talk about you, and add some words of persuasion,
    Let her swear that she knows you must be dying of love.
Hurry! before the sails are furled and the breezes grown milder;
    Anger, like brittle ice, dies with a little delay.
"Do you think it would do any good to seduce the maid?" What a
        question!
    Any such notions involve, always, too much of a risk.
One gets up from the bed too anxious, another too lazy,
    One aids her mistress's cause, one wants you all for her own.
Maybe it works, maybe not: it might be amusing to try it,
    Still, my advice would be, let it completely alone.
I would not show you the way over steep and precipitous passes,

No young man in my school ever will ride for a fall,
Yet, if she seems to please, while giving and taking your letters,
By her figure and face, not by her service alone,
Go for the lady first, and let the servant come second;
When you are making love, do not begin with the maid.
One final warning word: if you have any faith in my teaching,
If my words are not swept over the sea by the gale,
Either succeed, or don't try—she never will be an informer,
If she is guilty herself: how could she tattle on you?
Birds, with the lime on their wings, cannot take flight to the heavens,
Boars cannot plunge to their dens, caught in the mesh of the net.
Don't let your fish get away after the bait has been taken:
Press the attack, keep on; don't go away till you've won.
Then she can never betray you, because you were guilty together;
All of her mistress's acts, all of her words you will know.
Do not give her away: if she knows you are keeping her secrets,
She will be yours any time, knowing and willingly known.

It's a mistake to suppose that seasons are only for farmers
Toilsomely tilling the fields, only for seafaring men.
Seed should not always be sown, committed to treacherous acres,
Sails should not always be spread over the dark-green sea,
Nor is it always safe to go out hunting the darlings,
Often the thing is done better at suitable times.
If it's a birthday, let's say, or the feast of Venus in April,
When the Circus is dressed not with the usual signs,
That's a bad time; put it off—the omens are far from propitious,
Threatening weather lowers; you will be wrecked if you sail.
You can begin again on the day of the Allian battle
When that river ran red, swollen with Latian blood,
And one more possible time is the Palestinian Sabbath,
Not quite as good as the first, better than birthdays, by far.
Birthdays are worst of all: shun them with utter abhorrence,
Count it a black day indeed when you have presents to give.

Dodge this as well as you can, but still she will capture her plunder:
　　Women have ways; they know how they can swindle a man.
There will some peddler come by, a slovenly kind of a fellow,
　　Spreading his wares in her sight; she, in a purchasing mood,
Will ask you, poor wretch, to inspect them, making you think
　　　　you're an expert,
　　Then she will give you a kiss, then she will ask you to buy.
This will be all, she will swear, for many and many a season,
　　This is something she needs, now is a good time to buy.
If you make an excuse, and say that you've no money with you,
　　Give him a check, she will say: why did you learn how to write?
Often she'll wheedle for cash, *to buy a cake for her birthday.*
　　(She would be born once a month if it would suit her demand.)
She will pretend to be sad, and complain that she's lost something
　　　　precious,
　　Maybe a ring, or a gem slipped from the lobe of her ear.
Many things they will beg as a loan, and never return them:
　　You get no credit for this; whatever happens, you lose.
I could not possibly count the gold-digging ruses of women,
　　Not if I had ten mouths, not if I had ten tongues.

Let the tablets of wax prepare the way for your coming,
　　Let the tablets of wax indicate what's in your mind.
Let them carry sweet words, and every device of a lover,
　　And, whoever you are, do not forget to implore.
Priam's imploring prevailed, and Achilles returned Hector's body;
　　Even an angry god listens, attentive to prayer.
See that you promise: what harm can there be in promising freely?
　　There's not a man in the world who can't be rich in that coin.
Hope endures a long time, if once she has gained any credit;
　　She is a goddess indeed, useful, though apt to deceive.
Once you have made your gift, you can just as well be forsaken—
　　That's water over the dam, that hasn't cost her a cent,
But the gift not made, the gift of the possible future,

Like the barren field, fooling the husbandman's hope,
Like the gambler's bet, made to recover his losses
     When his covetous hands cannot let go of the dice,
That is the toil and the task, to keep her hoping for something—
     Keep her giving, lest she think she has given for free.
So, let your letter be sent, with coaxing words on the tablets,
     Make the reconnaissance first, scouting the pathways of love.
Think of Cydippe's vow, and the letter concealed in the apple,
     How that maiden was bound, speaking the words she had read.

Young men of Rome, I advise you to learn the arts of the pleader,
     Not so much for the sake of some poor wretch at the bar,
But because women are moved, as much as the people or Senate,
     Possibly more than a judge, conquered by eloquent words,
But dissemble your powers, and don't attempt to look learnèd,
     Let your periods shun rancorous terms of abuse.
You would be out of your mind to go and declaim to your darling;
     Even in letters beware using litigious terms.
Let the style you employ be natural, easy, familiar,
     Coaxing, also, of course, so that she thinks you are there.
If she refuses to read, or sends back a letter unopened,
     Hope that some day she will read, don't be discouraged. Some
          day!
Time brings the obdurate ox to submit to the yoke and the plough-
          share,
     Time brings the fieriest steed under the bridle and rein.
Even an iron ring is worn by continual usage,
     Even the hardest ground crumbles at last from the plough.
What is harder than rock, or what more gentle than water?
     Yet the water in time hollows the rigidest stone.
Only persist: you can have more luck than Penelope's suitors.
     Though it took a long time, Troy came tumbling down.
What if she reads, and won't answer? Do not attempt any pres-
          sure.

Only supply her with more flattering missives to read.
What she is willing to read, some day she'll be willing to answer—
    Every thing in its time, every thing by degrees.
Maybe the first response will make you sad by its scolding,
    Saying, "Don't write any more!", saying, "Please let me alone!"
What she requests, that she fears; what she does not ask, she in-
    sists on,
    So, go on with your work; some day the day will be won.

Meanwhile, if she is borne through the streets on a litter with
    cushions,
    Go to her side, but take care—don't give your mission away.
Hide what you really mean in cunning, equivocal language,
    Don't let anyone hear words that might cause him offense.
Or if she loiters afoot, by the colonnades and the porches,
    Dawdle along near by, either ahead or behind,
Or, now and then, cut across, if the columns are rising between you,
    With no apparent design, take a few steps at her side.
Also, be sure to be near when she sits in the theater watching;
    You will have something to watch, her shoulders, the curve of
    her dress.
Watch her as much as you please—you may turn around to admire
    her,
    There is a lot you can say, speaking with gesture and eye.
Clap and applaud when the star mimics a girl with his dancing,
    Favor the lover's cause—that's all that counts in the play.
When she rises, you rise; sit still, as long as she's seated;
    You have plenty of time, waste it to go with her whim.

Don't be crimping your locks with the use of the curling iron,
    Don't scrape the hair off your legs, using the coarse pumice
    stone;
Leave such matters as those to the members of Cybele's chorus,
    Howling their bacchanal strains under the dark of the moon.

Men should not care too much for good looks; neglect is becoming.
    Theseus, wearing no clasp, took Ariadne away,
Phaedra burned for his son, who was never exactly a dandy,
    Adonis, dressed for the woods, troubled a goddess with love.
Let your person be clean, your body tanned by the sunshine,
    Let your toga fit well, never a spot on its white,
Don't let your sandals be scuffed, nor your feet flap around in them
    loosely,
    See that your teeth are clean, brush them a least twice a day,
Don't let your hair grow long, and when you visit a barber,
    Patronize only the best, don't let him mangle your beard,
Keep your nails cut short, and don't ever let them be dirty,
    Keep the little hairs out of your nose and your ears,
Let your breath be sweet, and your body free from rank odors,
    Don't overdo it; a man isn't a fairy or tart.

Bacchus calls to his bards, and Bacchus calls to the lover:
    There is the god whose fire kindles the flame in the heart.
There is a story to prove it: Ariadne on Naxos,
    Wandering, out of her mind, over the desolate sands,
Just as she came from sleep, her garments loosened, and barefoot,
    Weeping, calling a name, *Theseus!* waves could not hear.
Weeping and calling she went, but her tears and her cries were
    becoming,
    Nor was there any disgrace in all the sorrow she bore.
Beating her gentle breast, she cried, "He has gone, he has left me,
    Left me forsaken, and gone: what will become of me now,
What will become of me now?" and heard, in answer, the cymbals
    Sounding along the shore, heard the beat of the drums
Beaten by frenzied hands, broke off her words, and in terror
    Fell to the ground in a swoon, whiter than Parian stone.
And here the Bacchanals came, their tresses streaming behind them,
    Here the Satyrs came, romping ahead of the god,
Here old Silenus came, drunk, on his sway-backed burro,

Hanging on for dear life, bouncing, and grabbing the mane,
Chasing the Bacchanals, and the Bacchanals fled, or attacked him
    While he still thought he could ride, prodding his mount with
        the goad;
There he goes over the side! and the Satyrs come rushing to help
    him,
    "Come on, Dad, you're all right; come on, old-timer, get up!"
Then comes the god in his car, with the clusters of grapes hanging
    over,
    Holding the reins of gold, driving the tigers along,
And there was the girl who had lost her voice, her color, her Theseus,
    Trying, three times, to escape, failing, three times, in her fear,
Shuddering, as dry stalks shiver in wind's agitation,
    Shuddering, as light reeds move in the wind by a stream,
Heard the god speak: "I am here for you, a lover more faithful:
    Daughter of Minos, be brave; take the gift of the sky;
You shall be mine, you will be adored as a star in the heaven
    And your diadem guide sailors in trouble at sea."
Then, lest the girl be afraid of the tigers, he leaped from the chariot,
    Came to her side on the sand, lifted her, bore her away
(She had no strength to fight back), and he clasped her close to his
    bosom—
    Gods do not find it hard, ever, to do as they will.
Then the crying arose: "Hail, Bacchus! Hail, Hymenaeus!"
    So are the god and his bride joined on the marriage-bed.

So, when the wine-god's grace has honored you with his blessing,
    And a woman lies sharing a part of your bed,
Pray to the god of the night, and all of the spirits of night-time,
    Not to permit the gift to go too much to your head.
But, before that, you must say words of ambiguous meaning,
    Messages meant for her ear; she can interpret the code.
Trace on the table in wine the flattering sketch or the symbol,
    So she may read and infer you are devoted to her.

Let your eyes gaze into hers, let the gazing be a confession:
Often the silent glance brings more conviction than words.
Be the first one to seize the cup that her lips have been touching,
Drink from that edge of the rim which she has touched with
her lips,
Ask her to pass the bread or the fruit she has touched with her
fingers;
When she passes it on, manage to touch her hand.
Also, make it your aim to get her husband to like you;
If you can make him your friend, he will be useful, you'll find.
If you are drinking by lot, and your turn comes first, let him have it,
Give him your garland to wear, say how becoming it seems.
No matter where he may sit, be sure that he has the first serving;
If he wants to hold forth, don't interrupt, let him talk.
Safe is the way, and well-worn, that takes advantage of friendship;
This is a way of guilt, safe though it be, and well-worn.
So a caretaker takes great care, and only too often
Takes more things than care, looks after more than his own.

Now, let me give you advice on the limit to put on your drinking:
Never let feet or mind either lose track of their place.
By all means avoid the quarrels that rise from the wine cup,
Only one thing is worse—fighting, resorting to blows.
Stupid Eurytion fell from too much drinking of liquor;
Let the food and the wine make you lighthearted and gay.
Sing, if you have any voice, or dance, if you're not too ungraceful,
Use any talent you have; only endeavor to please.
Getting really drunk is bad, but pretending to do so
Does no harm at all, might, in fact, be a gain.
Make your cunning tongue stumble and stutter a little,
So, if you go too far, people will say, "Oh, he's drunk."
Propose "A health to the lady! A health to the fellow she sleeps
with!"
Making your silent toast, "Damn her husband to hell!"

123

After the party breaks up, draw close to her in the confusion,
    Let your foot touch hers, finger the sleeve of her dress.
Now is the time for talk! Don't be an oaf of a farmer,
    Awkward, abashed, ashamed—Venus favors the bold!
Never mind learning the tropes, or the arts of verse composition,
    Only begin, that's all; eloquence comes as you plead.
Play the role of the lover, give the impression of heartache;
    No matter what your device, that you must make her believe,
Nor is it very hard—they all of them think that they're lovely,
    Even the ugliest hag dotes on her beauty's appeal.
More than once, you will find, the pretense ends in conviction,
    More than once the romance proves, after all, to be true.
So, girls, don't be too harsh on the men you suspect of pretending:
    Some day the butterfly, Truth, breaks from the lying cocoon.
Flattery works on the mind as the waves on the bank of a river:
    Praise her face and her hair; praise her fingers and toes.
Even honest girls are pleased if you broadcast their beauties,
    Even a virgin enjoys thinking herself a delight.
Why do you think to this day Juno and Pallas are grieving
    Over the verdict they lost on the far Phrygian coast?
Praise the peacock: at once she spreads her plumes in her pleasure.
    Watch, but say nothing at all: she'll keep her treasure concealed.
Horses, vying in speed around the curves of the race track,
    Proud of the well-groomed manes, cherish the pat on the neck.

Don't, when you promise, be shy; it takes many a promise to win them.
    Call, as your witnesses, such of the gods as you please.
Jupiter, high in the sky, laughs at the vows of false lovers,
    Orders the sweeping winds, "Carry those light vows away!"
Jupiter swore to his queen by the Styx, and knew he swore falsely,
    Now he looks down and approves of the example he set.
Gods are convenient to have, so let us concede their existence,

Bring to their obsolete shrine plenty of incense and wine.
Nor are they careless, aloof, calm in the semblance of slumber:
    Live an innocent life; godhead is certainly near.
Keep true faith, and return whatever is placed in your keeping;
    Keep your hands clean of blood; never indulge in a fraud.
If you are wise, you will know the rules permit one exception,
    One and one alone—only the girls are fair game.
Cheat these little cheats, for most of them haven't a scruple—
    Let them be caught in the net they are so eager to set.
Once, when Egypt lacked rain, the boon of the life-giving water,
    When the fields had been dry through nine terrible years,
Thracius went to Busiris, and said that the blood of a stranger
    Ought to be shed for relief; that would propitiate Jove,
And Busiris replied: "Very good, and you will redeem us,
    Stranger, yourself; your blood, victim, will water our land."
What Perillus designed, the bull for the rites of atonement,
    Phalaris first employed on the inventor himself.
Each of the two was just: contrivers of deadly devices
    Perish by their own arts—that is an absolute law.
So, as I said before, it is right to deceive the deceivers,
    Right that the woman should grieve, feeling the wound that
       she gives.

Tears are a good thing, too; they move the most adamant natures.
    Let her, if possible, see tears on your cheeks, in your eyes.
This is not easy: sometimes the eyes will not stream at your bid-
      ding.
    What can be done about this?—get your hands wet, and apply.
If you are wise, with your words include a proportion of kisses.
    She may not give in return; take, and pretend that she gives.
She may fight back at first, and call you all kinds of a villain;
    That is the kind of a fight she will be happy to lose.
Only don't hurt her too much; be big and strong, but be gentle;
    Don't let your roughness supply even the slightest excuse.

Once you have taken a kiss, the other things surely will follow,
    Or, if they don't, you should lose all you have taken before.
How far away is a kiss from the right true end, the completion?
    Failure the rest of the way proves you are clumsy, not shy.
Force is all right to employ, and women like you to use it;
    What they enjoy they pretend they were unwilling to give.
One who is overcome, and, suddenly, forcefully taken,
    Welcomes the wanton assault, takes it as proof of her charm.
But if you let her go untouched when you could have compelled her,
    Though she pretends to be glad, she will be gloomy at heart.
Phoebe, Hilaira, we know, were ravished by Pollux and Castor;
    Castor and Pollux, it seems, each proved a maiden's delight.
There is another old tale, familiar, but worth telling over,
    How, on Scyros, a maid joined with Achilles in love.
That was after the time of the triumph of Venus on Ida,
    Helen had come to Troy, Paris been given his bribe,
All of the Greeks (save one) sworn to revenge for the husband,
    Joined in a common cause over the grief of their king,
All of the Greeks save one, Achilles, who, heeding his mother,
    Hid in a shameful disguise, wearing the dress of a girl.
What did he have to do with weaving the wool, and with spinning?
    Pallas had other arts better devised for his fame.
What were baskets to him, whose arm should fit to the shield-strap?
    Why was a skein in the hand meant to bring Hector to doom?
Throw that spindle away, and all that nonsense, Achilles!
    What is your right hand for? Brandish the terrible spear!
Well, as it happened, a girl, Deidamia, shared the same bedroom;
    She was the one whom rape taught he was really a man.
She was taken by force, by violence—we must believe it—
    Still, being taken by force she had achieved her desire.
More than once she would cry, "Stay!" when Achilles was leaving
    (He had taken his arms, leaving the distaff and wool).
Where was the violence now, or the talk of rape, when she held him
    Close to her side as she could, coaxing with wheedling appeal?

Oh, of course, it's a shame to be the first one to start it,
    Still, when another one starts, isn't it fun to give in?
Nevertheless, young man, you'll be conceited and foolish
    If you wait till the girl makes the first passes at you.
Let the man be the first to make the approach and entreaty,
    Let the girl be the one willing to wait and be kind.
Ask her outright: that's all any girl has been waiting for, really,
    Give her a cause, an excuse, just so you give her a start.
Jove himself would go and beg the girls for their favors:
    He was seducer, in love; no girl solicited Jove.
Yet, if you find that your pleas inspire an arrogant coldness,
    Stop what you may have begun, take a few steps in retreat.
Many a girl desires the coy and hates the aggressive:
    Take it a little bit slow, don't let her weary of you.
Don't always show in your talk that you know you are going to get
        her—
    What you are eager to be, tell her, is *Only a friend.*
I have seen this work, on the most unwilling of women—
    Only a friend, who was found more than proficient in bed!

White is a color no sailor should have, but sunburnt from sea-wave,
    Sunburnt from wind and from star, that's how a sailor should be.
Farmers, too, should be brown from their work with ploughshare
        and harrow,
    Athletes tawny and dark, seeking their prize in the games,
But a pallor is right for the lover, a suitable color:
    Prithee, why not pale? that's the complexion for love.
Pale Orion went, walking the woodlands of Dirce;
    Pale was the shepherd-boy when his naiad was coy.
Thinness is also good, a proof of sentiment; also
    Do not think it a shame wearing a hood on your brow.
Lying awake all night wears down the bodies of lovers,
    All that passion and pain—how can you help but grow lean?

Be a pitiful sight, if it helps to accomplish your purpose,
    Let anyone who observes say, "The poor fellow's in love."

Now, should I warn, or complain, that right and wrong are confusing,
    Friendship an empty name, faith a delusion and snare?
This I hate to say: don't praise your girl to your best friend—
    Once he believes in your praise, he will sneak into your place.
"What!" you will say, "was Achilles ever betrayed by Patroclus?
    Were not the heroes all loyal and true to their own?"
Anyone hoping for this would expect that a larch would drop apples,
    Hunt for the hive of the bees out in the midst of a stream.
Only base actions please, and every man serves his own pleasure,
    Sweeter, perhaps, when it comes out of another man's pain.
Sad, but unhappily true, that an enemy isn't the danger
    When you're in love, but friends—those are the fellows to shun.
Brother or cousin, beware him; beware your "faithful Achates"!
    These are the ones you must watch, these are the ones you
        must fear.

I was about to conclude, but—the hearts of the girls! How they
        differ!
    Use a thousand means, since there are thousands of ends.
Earth brings forth varying yield: one soil is good for the olive,
    One for the vine, and a third richly productive in corn.
Hearts have as many moods as the heaven has constellations:
    He who is wise will know how to adapt to the mood.
Be like the Protean god, a wave, or a tree, or a lion,
    Fire, or shaggy boar, shifting to any disguise.
Some fish are taken with spears, and others taken by trolling,
    Some will rise to the fly, some must be hauled by the net.
Then there's the question of years, with experience also a factor;
    Wary, naïve—you must choose which is the method to use.
If you seem coarse to a prude, or learnèd to some little lowbrow,

She will be filled with distrust, made to feel cheap in your eyes,
So she will run away from an honest man, and go flying
    Off to the safer embrace of some inferior clown.

Part of my work remains, but a third of the labor is finished:
    Here let an anchor be thrown, holding my vessel secure.

BOOK

II

Give the victory cry, and give it over, and over!
    What I have sought, I have won: give the victory cry!
Happy, the lover brings green palms to the poem I have written:
    Homer and Hesiod yield, in his opinion, to me.
Paris was joyful, so, when he spread the sail from Amyclae,
    Bearing his stolen bride over the shine of the sea.
Pelops knew this mood when his car was triumphant in Elis,
    When his foreign wheels took Hippodamia home.
Not so fast, young man! Your vessel sails in mid-ocean,
    Far away, still, is the port; harbor and heaven are far.
It is by no means enough to have won your girl through my singing;
    What you have won by my art, art must instruct you to hold.
Seeking is all very well, but holding requires greater talent:
    Seeking involves some luck; now the demand is for skill.
Now, if ever, be kind, be gracious, Venus and Cupid,
    Favor my work, O Muse named for the power of love!
Great is the scope of my plan—to tell how to keep him a captive,
    Love, that vagabond boy, flitting all over the world.
He has two wings for his flight, he is fickle and light and capricious;
    Pinning his pinions down—that is the problem we face.

Minos, you may recall, had blocked the land and the water,
   Daedalus made his escape, bold in his path through the air.
Once the inventor contrived the labyrinth holding the monster,
   Bull and man in one, proving the guilt of the queen,
Then he spoke to the king: "Be kind to me, Minos the righteous:
   Let my exile end; let me return to my home.
There I might not live, because the fates were against me;
   There, in the land I love, let me be able to die.
Or let my son return, if his father's service is nothing;
   If you must keep the son, then let the father return."
That was all he said; he might have said more. To what purpose?
   Minos had less to say, only the one word, "No!"
When he knew the truth, he spoke again, but in secret,
   Spoke to his heart alone: "Daedalus, now is the time,
Use your master craft. Minos controls earth and ocean;
   Neither water nor land gives us a pathway of flight.
But the way of the sky is free, and we shall attempt it;
   Jove on high, be kind: favor my desperate aim.
Yours is the only way by which I can flee from the tyrant.
   I have in me no design on the bright stars of your crown.
If we could go by the Styx, we would swim the Stygian waters;
   I must devise new laws strange to the nature of man."
Troubles are good for the wits, for who would ever imagine
   Mankind could learn to rise, soaring the lanes of the air?
Daedalus fashioned wings, arranged the feathers in order,
   Bound them with linen and wax; soon the marvel was done.
Daedalus' son stood by, fooling with wax and the feathers,
   Happy, like any boy, all unaware of the why.
Daedalus spoke: "My son, those are the ships we must sail on,
   Those are our comfort, our aid, fleeing this tyrannous land.
Minos blocks everything else, but the air is not his dominion:
   There is our element; follow my art through the air.
But be careful; avoid the sight of Callisto, Orion,
   Keep your gaze away from the Great Wain and the Bear.

Follow me where I lead, as I go flying before you;
> You will be safe if you go following where I may lead,
For, if we go too high, toward the fierce and violent sunlight,
> The wax from the wings will dissolve under the heat of the air,
And if we go too low, too closely skimming the waters,
> Feathers will lose their lift, weighted by spray and by wave.
Fly between them both, and avoid the turbulence also,
> Where the breeze is light, son, let it bear you along."
With the advice he fits the wings to the boy, and he shows him
> How the wings should be moved, fledgling instruction in flight,
Then he puts on his own, attends to their careful adjustment,
> Hovers, a little afraid, for the new road of the air,
And, about to take off, remembers, and kisses the youngster—
> Once is hardly enough—and there are tears in his eyes.
There was a little hill, not half as big as a mountain,
> Rising above the plain; that was their launching-ground.
Daedalus, moving his wings, looked back to watch his companion,
> Held on his level course, both of them truly air-borne.
Now it's a wonderful way, and all the fear is forgotten;
> Icarus soars aloft, bolder, more proud of his skill,
While far off, far down, some angler, watching below them,
> Looks at the sky, and his hand almost lets go of the line.
Samos was off to their left; they had passed over Naxos and Paros,
> Passed over Delos, the isle where great Apollo was born.
On their right was Lebynthus, Calymne, dark with its woodland,
> Astypalae's fort, ringed with the fish-haunted seas,
When the boy, too bold, too young, too ambitious in daring,
> Forced his way too high, leaving his father below,
So the bonds of the wings were loosened, the fastenings melted,
> Nor could the moving arms hold in the desert of air.
Panic seized him: he stared from heaven's height at the water;
> In the rush of his fear, darkness brimmed in his eyes.
All of the wax was gone: his arms were bare as he struggled
> Beating the void of the air, unsupported, unstayed.

"Father!" he cried as he fell, "Oh, father, father, I'm falling!"
  Till the green of the wave closed on the agonized cry,
While the father, alas, a father no longer, was calling,
  "Icarus, where do you fly, Icarus, where in the sky?
"Icarus!" he would call—and saw the wings on the water.
  Now earth covers his bones; now that sea has his name.

So, if King Minos could not control the wings of a mortal,
  Why should a poet essay holding the wings of a god?
It's a delusion and snare to resort to Thessalian magic,
  No use at all the charm snatched from the brow of the foal.
None of Medea's herbs can keep a passion from dying,
  Nor are Marsian spells any more use in the end.
If incantations were sound, Medea would still be with Jason,
  Nor would Ulysses have left Circe's enamoring isle.
Philters are senseless, too, and dangerous; girls have gone crazy,
  Given a dose in disguise; philters can damage the brain.
Let unholy things be taboo. If you want her to love you,
  Be a lovable man; a face and a figure won't do.
You might have all the good looks that appealed to the sea-nymphs,
    or Homer;
  That's not enough, you will find; add some distinction of mind.
Beauty's a fragile boon, and the years are quick to destroy it,
  Always diminshed with time, never enduring too long.
Violets always fade, and the bloom departs from the lily;
  When the roses are gone, nothing is left but the thorn.
Look, my handsome young man, gray hairs will come in your life-
    time,
  Soon the wrinkles will plough furrows in cheek and in brow,
So, make a soul to endure, a spirit to go with the body;
  Spirit and soul will abide, up to the ultimate fire.
Culture is surely worth while, and the liberal arts are a blessing:
  Take some trouble to learn two great languages well.

THE ART OF LOVE

Handsome, Ulysses was not, but his eloquence charmed with its
     power
     Goddesses out of the sea, burning to grant him their love.
Ah, how often Calypso grieved at his threat of departure,
     Seeking to make him stay, saying the waves ran too high!
Over and over she begged to hear about Troy, all that story;
     Often he varied the words, telling the story again.
They had come down to the shore, and even there she persisted:
     "Tell of King Rhesus of Thrace, tell of his pitiful doom!"
He had a staff in his hand, and made a map for the story,
     Sketching a plan in the sand. "This," he would tell her, "is Troy.
Here is Simois' stream, and here is my camp; now imagine
     There is a plain near by—there we slew Dolon, the spy,
While he was lying in wait, and keeping his eye on the horses.
     Here were the tents of the king, during the night when I came
Riding his captured steeds—" There would have been more to the
     story,
     Only a sudden wave washed away horses and Troy,
Washed away Rhesus, the king; and Calypso saw her advantage:
     "How can you trust those waves? See what great names they
     destroy!"

So, whoever you are, place little reliance on beauty,
     Take some pains to acquire something beyond a physique.
Tactfulness, tolerance—these are more than desirable virtues.
     Harshness arouses hate, rancor, resentment, and war.
Why do we hate the hawk? Because he lives by aggression.
     Why do we hate the wolves, stalking the timorous fold?
But we set no snares for the swallow, because he is gentle,
     Set no snares for the dove, haunting the eaves of the tower.
Keep far away, far off, all bitter tongue-lashing quarrels;
     Love is a delicate thing, won with affectionate words.
Husbands and wives, by right, may harry each other with nagging;
     Let them believe, as they must, this is their nature and law.

This is all right for wives: the dower of a wife is a quarrel;
     Let your mistresses hear nothing but what they desire.
You have not come to one bed in the name of the law, but more
          freely.
     Love is your warrant and bond, love holds the office of law.
Bring her courtesies, and flattering words, and endearments,
     Words that are sweet to the ear; make her be glad you are there.
I do not lecture the rich in my role of professor of loving:
     If you have presents to bring, you have no need of my art.
"Here is something for you!" A man who can say that has genius!
     I give up, I retire; he can learn nothing from me.
I am a poor man's poet, because I was always a poor man;
     Loving, I made no gifts, only a present of words.
Poor men should watch their step and poor men should watch their
          language,
     Poor men should learn to bear more than the rich would endure.
I remember a time when I pulled my girl's hair in my anger:
     How many days did that cost? More than I like to recall.
I did not know that I tore her dress, and I still do not think so:
     Still, she said that I did; who do you think had to pay?
So, if you are wise, avoid the mistakes of your teacher,
     Let my experience help, save you both time and expense.
Fight with the Parthian hordes, but keep the peace with your lady,
     Have some fun, and enjoy all the inducements of love.
If she is somewhat rude, and none too polite to your loving,
     Stick it out, endure; one of these days she'll be kind.
Gently, gently move, when you try to bend the bough over:
     Don't make a show of your strength, or the bough will break in
          your hand.
Gently, gently float, and go along with the river:
     Rivers are not to be won forcing your way upstream.
Kindness, the trainers say, will tame even lions and tigers,
     Little by little the bull learns to submit to the plough.
Who could have been more tough, less yielding than Atalanta?

Yet in the end, as we know, she was compelled to give in.
Often Milanion wept, under the trees in the forest,
　　Mourning his desolate lot, mourning her merciless ways.
Often he carried the nets, as she told him to, on his shoulders,
　　Often his violent spear pierced to the heart of the boar.
Once he felt the wound of the arrow aimed by Hylaeus;
　　He knew another bow, Cupid's, more potent to harm.
Now, I don't tell you to go and sob in Maenalian forests,
　　I do not tell you to bear nets on your shoulders and back,
I do not tell you to bare your breast to a volley of arrows,
　　My admonition will be cautious and easy to heed.
Yield if she resists; if you yield, you will come away winner:
　　Only one thing you must do—what she is asking you to.
Blame whatever she blames; approve what meets her approval;
　　What she says you must say; what she denies, you deny.
Laugh when she laughs; if she weeps, remember to join her in weep-
　　　　ing;
　　Let her expression impose laws for your face to obey.
If she is throwing the dice, whatever the point she is making,
　　Talk to the dice as she rolls, hope she will pass every time.
When your turn comes around, it is better to be a good loser:
　　Let the snake-eyes fall; what do you care? After all!
Or if you're playing at chess, let her capture a few of your pieces,
　　Maybe a bishop or rook, let her cry "Mate!" at the end.
Carry her parasol (they're always a struggle to open,
　　Never mind that); be sure she can find room in a crowd.
Be on hand with a stool when she's taking her ease on the cushions,
　　Help her slip off her mules, help her, again, put them on.
Often, when she is cold, though you yourself are all shivers,
　　Hold her hands in your own, rub them to keep them warm.
Do not think it a shame (it is, but still it will please her)
　　That your hand, freeborn, holds up a mirror for her)
When his stepmother tired of sending threatening monsters,
　　Hercules, so they say, spun the Ionian wool,

Meeker than any girl—but he came at last to the heavens:
   Who do you think you are? greater than Hercules?
If she tells you to come to the forum, where she will meet you,
   Be there before she expects, linger long after the hour.
If it is somewhere else, postpone all other engagements,
   Run as fast as you can, don't let a crowd block your way.
When she comes home at night, after the party is over,
   If you should hear her call, hurry in place of her slave.
She may be out of town and say "Come!" Love despises the lazy;
   Maybe you haven't a car—then make the journey on foot.
Do not be delayed by storms, by the sultriest weather;
   Don't be reluctant to go when the road whitens with snow.

Love is a kind of war, and no assignment for cowards.
   Where those banners fly, heroes are always on guard.
Soft, those barracks? They know long marches, terrible weather,
   Night and winter and storm, grief and excessive fatigue.
Often the rain pelts down from the drenching cloudbursts of heaven,
   Often you lie on the ground, wrapped in a mantle of cold.
Did not Apollo once, in bondage to King Admetus,
   Care for the heifers, and find sleep on a pallet of straw?
What Apollo could stand is not disgraceful for mortals;
   Put off your pride, young man; enter the bondage of love.
If you are given no path where the journey is level and easy,
   If in your way you find barricade, padlock on door,
Use your inventive wits, come slipping down through a skylight,
   Clamber, hand over hand, where a high window swings wide.
She will be happy to know that she was the cause of your danger;
   More than anything else, that will be proof of your love.
Think of Leander, who could, no doubt, get along without Hero,
   Yet he would swim the straits, so his beloved might know.

Do not feel ashamed to win her serving-maids over,
   Take them according to rank; also, win over her slaves.
Greet each one by name—the courtesy can't be expensive—

Show them your *Noblesse oblige*, clasping their hands in your
   own.
If, on the Day of Good Luck, some slave should ask for a present,
   Give him some little gift; this should cost nothing at all.
On the Handmaidens' Day, recalling the Gauls and the fig tree,
   Think of the girls in the house, try to remember each one.
Take my advice: it is worth your while to be good to the lowly,
   Even the guard at her gate, even the slave at her door.
I do not say you should spend great sums on gifts for the lady:
   Let them, however small, seem to be chosen with care.
While the fields are rich, and the boughs droop under their burden,
   Have a boy come to the door, bringing her baskets of fruit.
Tell her they came from your farm, your little place in the country:
   She would not know, nor suspect fruit stands are easy to find.
Have the boy bring her grapes, or the nuts Amaryllis was fond of,
   Send her a thrush or a dove, proof of your passionate love.
But, don't send souvenirs suggestive of anything morbid,
   Death, or a childless old age, anything hinting of guilt.

What about sending her poems? A very difficult question.
   Poems, I am sorry to say, aren't worth so much in this town.
Oh, they are praised, to be sure; but the girls want something more
   costly.
   Even illiterates please, if they have money to burn.
Ours is a Golden Age, and gold can purchase you honors,
   All the "Golden Mean" means is, gold is the end.
Homer himself, if he came attended by all of the Muses,
   With no scrip in his purse, would be kicked out of the house.
There are a few, very few, bright girls with a real education,
   Some (perhaps) here and there, willing to give it a try.
So, go ahead, praise both: the worth of the song matters little
   Just so you make it sound lovely while reading aloud.
Whether or not she can tell one kind of verse from another,
   If there's a line in her praise she will assume, "It's a gift!"

What you were planning to do, provided it serves your advantage,
    Get her to think of first, get her to take the lead.
There may be one of your slaves, to whom you have promised his
        freedom;
    Have him appeal to her, give him the gift in her name.
If you release a slave from chains or the threat of a flogging,
    What you intended to do, make her beholden to you.
Make the gain your own, but let her have all of the credit;
    You lose nothing, and she gains in her sense of *largesse*.
But, whoever you are, if you're truly anxious to hold her,
    See that she thinks you are held, stunned by her beauty and
        charm.
If she's in Tyrian dress, then praise her Tyrian dresses;
    If in the Coan mode, say that the Coan is best.
Is she in gold? let her be more dear than her golden apparel;
    Is she in wool? approve woolen, becoming to her.
If she appears in her slip, cry out, "You inflame me with passion!"
    Ask, in a timid voice, "Aren't you afraid you'll be cold?"
Praise the new part in her hair, and praise the way she has curled it;
    Praise her dance and her song; cry "Encore!" at the end.
Also, her ways in bed you should speak of with adulation,
    Calling them out of this world, praising the joys of the night.
Though she is wild and fierce, untamed as any Medusa,
    She will be gentle and kind when the right lover is near.
Don't give yourself away, if you have to resort to deception,
    Don't let a gesture or look spoil the effect of your words.
Art is effective, concealed; but once it is out in the open
    Brings, as it should, disgrace, takes all your credit away.

Often in autumn time, the year's most beautiful season,
    When the cluster swells, full of the crimsoning wine,
When one day is cold, and the next is almost too sultry,
    In that uncertain air, languor takes hold of us all.
Pray that she keeps her health, but if she happens to lose it,

If she is ailing, and feels all the caprice of the sky,
Let her be perfectly sure of your constant love and devotion:
    Now, in the fall, you can sow what will be harvest in spring.
Patience! Take no offense at even her fretfullest symptoms;
    What she will let you do, be at her side to attend.
Let her see you in tears; don't weary of giving her kisses;
    Let her dry mouth drink teardrops that fall from your eyes;
Make many vows, all aloud; and whenever it suits your good pleas-
        ure,
    Tell her of healing dreams, bringing good omens at night;
Get some old woman to come, with sulphur and eggs for the bed-
        room,
    These are medicinal, both purification and cure.
All such solicitude will prove your attentive devotion;
    This is the path that leads straight to a clause in her will.
Yet, when a girl is sick, be careful, and don't overdo it:
    Keep your flattering zeal always within proper bounds.
Do not force her to fast, nor compel her to drink bitter doses;
    Let prescriptions like those be for your rival to urge.

Once you have spread your sail, and are over the deeps of the ocean,
    Bear in mind that the breeze differs from zephyrs at home.
While your love is young, let it err, but let it be learning.
    If you nourish it well, it will be healthy in time.
You fear, now, the bull you used to pet in its calfhood;
    Saplings, in time, become trees with a welcoming shade;
Rivers are small at their birth, but gain in the strength of their cur-
        rent,
    Taking, as on they run, many and many a stream.
Let her grow used to you: no force is greater than habit:
    Till you establish that, never be tired of the toil.
Always appear in her sight, and always contrive that she listen,
    Be a presence, on hand all of her nights and her days;
Don't stay away, not once, until you are sure she will miss you,

Don't go away till you know she will be sorry you go.
Then you can give her a rest: a field grows better when fallow;
    Thirsty, the dry soil thrives best in response to the rain.
Phyllis's ardor was mild, at least, in Demophoon's presence;
    When his sail was spread, then she broke out into flame.
So did Penelope fret, in the absence of crafty Ulysses;
    Protesilaus was gone, then Laodamia grieved.
Still, a short absence is best: be away too long, she'll forget you:
    Hearts are inclined to grow fond, then, of available men.
When Menelaus was gone, and the bed of Helen was lonesome,
    Paris and warmth were found in the embrace of the night.
Menelaus, I think, was a fool to go off on a journey,
    Leaving his wife and his guest housed in identical walls.
Only a madman would think that the dove was safe with the falcon,
    Only a madman leave sheep to the mercy of wolves.
Helen was not to blame, and neither, so help me, was Paris;
    Given the chance that he had, who would do anything else?
You were to blame, Menelaus: you gave him the time, the occasion;
    Why in the world should they not follow the counsel you gave?
What did you think she would do? Her husband was gone, she was
        lonely,
    Paris was far from a boor—why should she sleep all alone?
I acquit Helen outright, and put the blame on the husband.
    What did she do but make use of the occasion he gave?

No red raging boar is as fierce, in the foam of his anger,
    When his lightning tusks slash at the charge of the pack,
No lioness is as fierce, when her cubs are still at her udders,
    No blunt adder as fierce, trodden under the foot,
As a woman in love, when she learns that a rival has taken
    Part of the bed she has shared; see how her countenance burns!
Out of the house she will rush, for fire and sword in her frenzy,
    All of her decency gone, wild with a Bacchanal's rage.
Jason paid for his sin when Medea murdered the children;

Procne, a swallow now, holds the red stain on her breast.
This is the kind of crime that breaks the strongest attachment,
    This, above all, is the crime vigilant husbands should fear.
Yet far be it from me to say you should always be faithful.
    Heaven forbid! that would be more than a bride should require.
Play around, but take care to practice a decent concealment;
    Don't go bragging about, counting them up like Don Juan.
Don't give presents to one, if the news will get to the other;
    Don't have a definite time for your promiscuous fun;
Don't always go to one place, where somebody else might surprise
    you;
    When you send letters, be sure you've the right name and ad-
    dress.
Venus, when hurt, strikes back, a goddess vindictive and vengeful,
    Making you suffer the wound you were so ready to give.
While Agamemnon was true, Clytemnestra also was faithful;
    His was the sin that brought on her retribution and fall.
Had she not heard of that girl, the golden daughter of Chryses,
    Heard of Achilles' prize, Briseis, taking her place?
These she had heard of, no more, but she saw the daughter of Priam,
    Booty brought home from the wars, lording it over the king.
Not until then did she make her cousin, Aegisthus, her lover,
    Not until then was her sin conscious, an act of revenge.

If you are ever caught, no matter how well you've concealed it,
    Though it is clear as the day, swear up and down it's a lie.
Don't be too abject, and don't be too unduly attentive,
    That would establish your guilt far beyond anything else.
Wear yourself out if you must, and prove, in her bed, that you could
    not
    Possibly be that good, coming from some other girl.
Some recommend Spanish Fly as useful on such an occasion:
    This I do not endorse; I think it poison or worse.
Others say pepper is good, compounded with seeds of the nettle,

142

Or try a camomile brew, steeping pyrethrum in wine,
But I very much doubt whether these can be very effective:
  Venus will hardly respond, called to the usual joys.
Scallions might work, if you get the kind that are shipped from Meg-
      ara;
  Rocket and basil are good, culled from the gardens of home.
Also, eat plenty of eggs, and the honey that comes from Hymettus,
  Nuts from the long-leaved pine, oysters (in months with an R).

Why fool around with all this medicinal magic and nostrums?
  There is a better way; turn your direction, and heed.
Not long ago I said it was wise to dissemble your cheating,
  Now I reverse myself—let it be openly told.
Inconsistent? Of course, but is that any reason to scold me?
  Winds do not always blow from the same reach of the sky.
East, West, North, or South—and we plan our course in accordance.
  Drivers can hold the reins easy or tight at their will.
There are some girls who are bored with over-devoted indulgence:
  Given no rival, their love languishes, fades, dies away.
Spirit can grow too rank, when matters are going too smoothly,
  Nor is it easy to bear Fortune's continual smile.
Just as a fire dies down, and weakens, little by little,
  While the embers lie hid under the gray of the ash,
But if you rouse the flame, half-dead, by throwing on sulphur,
  Then it flares up again, brighter in light than before.
So, when hearts grow dull with too much freedom from worry,
  They must be given the spur, given incentive to love.
Heat her cooling mind, and let her grow anxious about you:
  Let her grow pale when she hears evidence you are untrue.
Lucky beyond all count is the man whom a woman grieves over,
  Pales at the word of his wrong, falls in a faint to the ground.
I would not mind, in that case, if she tried to snatch me bald-headed,
  Tore at my cheeks with her nails, frantic and weeping with rage,
Gave me her angriest looks, and wanted to do what she could not,

Namely, live without me—what an impossible hope!
If you should ask me, "How long is a suitable time for resentment?"
    I would say, Not too long; anger flares up with delay.
While she is still in tears, put your arms gently around her,
    While she is still in tears, hold her close to your breast,
Give her, while still in tears, kisses, and something much better—
    That is the only way; anger succumbs to that peace.
When she has raged her fill, and seems an enemy, surely,
    Take her to bed; you will find she will be gentle and mild.
There the arms are laid down in favor of concord and union;
    There, you can take it from me, harmony truly is born.
The doves, who were lately at war, join bill to bill in affection;
    Soft is the *roucoulade*, murmuring, cooing of love.

First there was Chaos, the Void, a rude and shapeless confusion,
    Earth and the stars and the seas none from the other apart.
Presently sky was set over earth, and earth girded with water,
    All things came to their place, Chaos withdrew from the world.
Forests sheltered the beasts, the birds wheeled high in the heaven,
    Fish found their watery home deep in the caverns of sea.
Then the human race wandered in desolate acres,
    Men were alone and lost, brutal and graceless, but strong.
Woods were their home, and grass their food, and leaves were their
        bedding;
    None of them seemed to know creatures after his kind.
Somehow, they learned of a pleasure, to tame their truculent spirits;
    Somehow, a woman and man stayed in one place for a while.
What they did, they learned without a master to teach them;
    Sweet was the artless work, urged by the goddess of love.
Birds found birds to love, and fishes mated with fishes,
    Serpent with serpent joined, the buck and the doe were one,
Heifers were glad of the bull, and the mares would follow the stud-
        horse
    Wild with desire, and no stream ever would stand in their way.

Need I say more? You should know the cure when a woman is angry.
　　Bring the specific she needs, warrant of rest and repose.
You have medicinal arts beyond the lore of Machaon;
　　You should know what to apply when you are fallen from grace.

While I was singing this song, I saw, of a sudden, Apollo,
　　Clear in the golden light, sweeping the strings of his lyre.
Laurel was in his hands, and his hair was crowned with the laurel,
　　Poet from head to foot, something for eyes to behold!
"Bring your pupils to me," he said, "O wanton instructor!
　　In my shrine is a phrase known all over the world.
Know thyself, it says; and no man can ever love wisely,
　　Without knowing himself, no man can be at his best.
If nature gave you good looks, then do your best to display them;
　　If you are tanned by the sun, show an abundance of skin.
If you can please by your talk, avoid long pauses and silence;
　　If you're a singer, sing; if you're a drinker, drink.
But, don't interrupt when a clever person is talking—
　　Also, unless you're mad, don't read poems of your own!"
That was Apollo's advice, and very good counsel to follow:
　　Words from the mouth of that god all of us surely can trust.

I am called closer home. The man who learns to love wisely,
　　Taught by my art, may be sure he will win out in the end.
Soil does not always return the favoring interest of harvest;
　　Wind does not always propel ships on a prosperous course.
Little there is to help, and much to injure, a lover:
　　Let him make up his mind he will have much to endure.
Many as hares on Mount Athos, or bees in the valley of Hybla,
　　Many as fruits that bend boughs of the gray olive-trees,
Many as shells on the shore are the troubles that irritate lovers:
　　Our frustrations are barbs, steeped in the bitterest gall.
She will be said to be "out," when you know she's at home; you have
　　　　seen her.

145

Best to believe she is out; don't take the word of your eyes.
The door will be locked in your face on the night she gave you her
      promise;
      Patience and fortitude! Sleep on the ground at her door.
Maybe some lying maid, with the nastiest kind of expression,
      Comes to the door and remarks, "Why is this mendicant here?"
Say your prayers to the door, and say your prayers to the handmaid,
      Hang on the post of the door roses removed from your brow.
Come when she wants you to come; when she avoids you, be going.
      No man of breeding can bear ever becoming a bore.
Never let her say, "I can't get rid of this fellow!"
      What do you think she is—always in passionate mood?
Do not think it a shame to suffer her blows or her curses;
      Do not think it a shame, stooping, to kiss her feet.

Why do I talk about trifles, with greater matters before me?
      Great is my theme; come close, listen with all your heart.
This is a difficult task, but manliness faces the challenge;
      Difficult tasks are required if you would learn from my art.
Patience and fortitude! Suppose you do have a rival,
      Victory comes to the brave; wait and endure, you will win!
Trust this word of advice, as if it came from Dodona,
      Nothing in all I have said has more importance than this:
If she beckons, respond; let her alone if she's writing;
      Let her come and go whence and wherever she will.
Even husbands extend this much to the wives of their bosom,
      They concede this much, anyway when they're asleep.
In this art, I admit, I am far, myself, from perfection:
      What can I do about this? Practice my preaching, I guess.
When I am there at her side, with somebody giving her signals,
      This I should bear, I suppose? not lash myself into rage?
Once, I recall, she was given a kiss, just a peck, by her husband;
      I complained of the kiss—what a barbarian boor!
More than once, I am sure, this fault has been my undoing:

Wiser the man whose consent leads to the opening door.
Not to know is the best; let her deceptions be hidden;
    When she would blush to confess, let her spare blushes, and
        hide.
So, young man, all the more, don't catch your girls when they're
        cheating:
    Let them behave as they will, let them think nobody knows.
Once they are caught, love grows: with two guilty parties to deal
        with,
    Each persists all the more, proud of his fate and his fall.
Everyone knows the tale, told over and over in Heaven,
    All about Vulcan's net, capturing Venus and Mars.
Father Mars, driven wild by a frantic passion for Venus,
    Changed from a captain of war into a captive of love,
Nor was Venus averse (no goddess was ever more willing),
    Neither bashful nor coy in her response to his prayer.
How many times she is said to have laughed at the limp of her
        husband,
    Laughed at Vulcan's hands, calloused from work at the forge!
Mars would enjoy and approve her imitations of Vulcan;
    Beauty and wit combined in her seductive appeal.
In the first stages, their loves were hidden by artful concealment,
    Guilt had a sense of shame, modesty made its pretense.
Who can deceive the Sun? The Sun-god informed on the lovers,
    Vulcan was told of it all—what an example to set!
Better, I think, to keep still, to suggest, in return for his silence,
    Favors she surely would grant, only too glad to oblige.
So, around their bed, and over it, Vulcan with cunning,
    Spread the invisible snares, meshes too fine for the eye,
Left for Lemnos (he said), and the lovers rushed to their meeting—
    There, in the toils of the nets, naked and taken they lie.
Vulcan summons the gods—an Olympian spectacle, truly!—
    Venus in tears, and Mars hiding his tool with his hand.
Somebody, laughing, cried out, "Oh Mars, most valiant of heroes,

If the chains are too much, why not transfer them to me?"
Neptune said, "Let them go," and Vulcan, still grudging, relented,
    Mars hurried off to Thrace, she to her Paphian isle.
That was by no means the end: what they concealed, at the outset,
    They do more freely now, everyone knowing their shame.
Vulcan himself, they say, admitted his foolishness later,
    Called himself stupid and mad, many and many a time.
This is a lesson for all: be warned by what happened to Venus;
    Don't fashion any such snare; think what she had to endure;
Don't try to spring any traps for your rival, don't intercept letters—
    That's for a husband to do, not for a lover like you.
Once again I repeat: the game is perfectly legal,
    Nothing but good clean fun; don't be a judge in a gown.

Who would dare to expose the ceremonies of Ceres,
    Who profane the rites held on the sanctified ground?
Silence is little enough, a negative kind of a virtue;
    Blabbing the mysteries—what an unspeakable crime!
Tantalus talked too much, and deserves to stretch for the apples
    Always out of his reach, thirsting, with water around.
Venus expressly forbids her sacred rites to be broadcast;
    To her service, I warn, let no tattletale come.
Not in boxes of bronze are her sacred mysteries hidden;
    Free for our daily use, they should be given their due,
Modestly covered, as Venus herself will cover her secrets,
    Bending with left hand low, seen in the statue's pose.
Only the animals mate where everybody can see them—
    Often a modest girl turns her eyes from the sight.
Bedrooms and bolted doors are the place for our intimate unions;
    Even there we can lie under the covering sheet,
Even there we prefer, if not an absolute darkness,
    Shadow, half-light, a shade, not the full blaze of the sun.
In the old primitive days, when the sun and the rain were prevented
    Not by the sheltering roof, only by pine-tree and oak,

People made love in groves, in caves, not out in the open;
    Even the primitive folk recognized decency's claim.
Now we make great boasts of the feats we perform in the night-time,
    Prize, more than anything else, loosing extravagant talk.
Everyone has to try to make every girl in the city,
    Telling whoever you please, "I have been sleeping with her,"
So there will be no lack of girls for a finger to point at,
    So there will be no girl out of the reach of your tale.
This is a minor offense: some will go very much farther,
    Saying there's no one in town they haven't had in their time.
Bodies they cannot touch, at least they can handle by naming;
    Bodies they could not touch, they can lay claim to in talk.
Go now, hateful guard, barricade the doors of a lady,
    On the resolute posts placing your bolts by the score!
What is the good of all this, if any concupiscent liar
    Enters in fancy, his wish making adultery true?
I, for my part, believe my affairs are entirely my business;
    What I have done in the dark adamant secrecy hides.

Do not blame a girl for flaws of her nature or person:
    Where's the advantage in that? Better pretend them away.
Andromeda, it would seem, was none too fair of complexion;
    Perseus, the sandal-winged, never voiced any reproach.
All thought Andromache was much too big for a woman;
    Only in Hector's eyes was she of moderate size.
If you like what you get, you will get what you like; love is captious
    In our salad days, growing more mellow in time.
While the grafted shoot is new in the green of its growing,
    Even the lightest breeze makes it shudder and fall,
But it will fasten with time, so even a gale cannot shake it,
    Bear, on the parent tree, increase after its kind.
Time is a healer, and time removes all faults from the body;
    What was a blemish of old comes to be nothing at all.
When we are children, we find the odor of leather obnoxious,

Hardly can stand it at all; when we are grown, we don't mind.
Words have a magical power to mitigate many shortcomings:
    If she is blacker than tar, *tanned* is the term to employ.
Cross-eyed? She looks like Venus! Albino? Fair as Minerva!
    Thin as a rail? What grace lies in her willowy charm!
If she's a runt, call her *cute*; if fat, *a full-bodied woman*:
    Dialectic can make grace out of any defect.

Don't ask her when she was born, or under whose administration:
    That's for the censor to do, leave the statistics to him.
All the more, if she's past the bloom of her youth, in her thirties,
    Plucking out whitening hairs, scanning her mirror for more.
That's a good age, young man, and even a little bit older,
    That's a field that will bear, that's a field to be sown.
Keep at the task for a while, as long as your vigor permits it;
    All too soon old age, silent, comes limping along.
Plough the sea with your oars, or furrow the land with your
        ploughshare,
    Take your warlike tools for the fierce hazards of war,
Or devote to the girls your strength, your vigor of body,
    This is a kind of war, this makes demands on your power.
Don't forget, the mature have greater skill in the business:
    What experience brings, they are adept to employ.
They have the talent, the knack, to turn the years to advantage,
    They are proficient, adroit; they know how not to seem old.
They know a thousand ways of love, however you like it,
    They do not need any book, "What a Young Girl Ought to
        Know."
They do not need to be teased, to be worked up into a frenzy,
    They can keep up with a man—yes, and a good thing, too.
What I like is the deal that leaves both partners exhausted;
    That's why I find no joy in the embrace of a boy.
What I hate is the girl who gives with a feeling she has to,
    Dry in the bed, with her mind somewhere else, gathering wool.

Duty is all very well, but let's not confuse it with pleasure;
　　I do not want any girl doing her duty for me.
What I like to hear are the words of utter abandon,
　　Words that say, "Not too soon!", words that say, "Wait just a
　　　　while!"
Let me see my girl with eyes that confess her excitement;
　　Let her, after she comes, want no more for a while.
What does youth know of delight? Some things ought not to be
　　　　hurried;
　　After some thirty-odd years, lovers begin to learn how.
Let the premature guzzle wine that is hardly fermented,
　　I'll take wine from a jar mellowed in vintage with time.
Only the full-grown tree resists the heat of the sunlight,
　　Meadows too recently sown offer the barefoot no joy.
Who wants Hermione, if Helen is his for the taking?
　　Look for a woman, mature, not any slip of a girl.
Love is an art learned late, but if you are willing, and patient,
　　Playing your part like a man, you will have fitting reward.

Now the bed has received two lovers; the bed seems to know it.
　　Now the door has been closed; linger, O Muse, at the door.
They will not need you, now, for the words they will whisper and
　　　　murmur,
　　Nor will the left hand lie idle along the bed.
Fingers will find what to do in those parts where love plies his
　　　　weapons:
　　Hector could use his hands in more endeavors than war,
So could Achilles, who lay with the captive from Lyrna beside him,
　　Tired from the wars, but a man in the soft ease of the bed.
Briseis did not object when his hands moved over her body,
　　Hands that had always known slaughter and Phrygian blood.
Or was it this, just this, that heightened her sense of excitement,
　　Feeling a conqueror's hands come to her secretest parts?
Take my word for it, love is never a thing to be hurried,

Coax it along, go slow, tease it with proper delay.
When you have found the place where a woman loves to be fondled,
    Let no feeling of shame keep your caresses away.
Then you will see in her eyes a tremulous brightness, a glitter,
    Like the flash of the sun when the water is clear.
She will complain, but not mean it, murmuring words of endearment,
    Sigh in the sweetest way, utter appropriate cries.
Neither go too fast, nor let her get there before you;
    Pleasure is best when both come at one time to the goal.
Slow is the pace to keep when plenty of leisure is given,
    When you can dally at ease, free from the pressure of fear,
But when delay is not safe, it is useful to drive with full power,
    Useful to give your mount spirited prick of the spur.

Here is the end of my work: be thankful, bring me the laurel,
    Bring me the palm, young men, grateful for what I have taught.
The Greeks had their heroes of old, their specialists, Nestor in counsel,
    Ajax, Achilles, in arms, wily Ulysses in guile,
Calchas, prophetic seer, and Podalirius, healer,
    Automedon in his car—I am the master in love.
Give me your praises, men: I am your poet, your prophet;
    Let my name be known, lauded all over the world.
I have given you arms, as Vulcan gave arms to Achilles,
    Now that the gift is made, conquerors, go to the wars!
But if your shaft lays low your Amazonian victims,
    Write on the votive spoil, "Ovid showed me the way."

Look! The girls are here, and asking me for some lessons.
    You will be next, my dears: turn the page to Book Three.

BOOK

III

I gave arms to the Greeks against the Amazon forces:
 Arms for the Amazons now; turn about is fair play.
Go to the wars, well-matched, and win by the blessing of Venus,
 Win by the grace of her son, flying all over the world.
It would be most unfair for the naked to fight men in armor;
 That is no victory, men; you would regard it with shame.
I can hear somebody say: "Are you furnishing serpents with poison,
 Turning the mad she-wolves loose on the innocent fold?"
Don't impute to them all the crimes of a few wicked women;
 Give a fair hearing to all, let their merits decide.
If Menelaus had good warrant for railing at Helen,
 If Agamemnon's queen killed in adulterous lust,
If Amphiaraus drove his car to the Stygian caverns,
 Through Eriphyle's crime, bought with a necklace of gold,
Did not Penelope keep true faith while her crafty Ulysses
 Fought ten years in the war, added ten wandering years?
Think of Alcestis, who gave her days for the life of Admetus,
 Think of Evadne's love, true in the flames of the pyre.
Virtue herself is portrayed in modest robes, as a woman;
 Virtue, in modest white, has her own people to please.
Leave her subjects to her: I make no claim on her province;

My diminutive craft speeds with the slightest of sail.
I teach nothing but love, in its naughtier manifestations—
     How should a woman be loved? Ovid will show you the way.
Women do not hurl flames, nor aim any venomous arrows,
     Seldom I see their arms torturing innocent men.
Men are the ones who deceive, men are continual liars;
     Search for deceitful girls, they are not easy to find.
Jason's perfidy doomed Medea, already a mother,
     When the second bride came to his eager embrace.
Theseus abandoned a girl to the lonely shores of the sea birds,
     Ariadne was left fearful on Naxos, alone.
Ask why they call one way Nine Ways, and learn about Phyllis,
     Losing Demophoon, left, pitiful even to trees.
Pious Aeneas we know, that guest with the great reputation,
     Leaving to Dido the sword, leaving the cause of her doom.
What destroyed them all? Nothing but ignorant loving,
     They were unversed in the art; love requires art to survive.
I would let them alone, but Venus has bidden me teach them,
     Venus herself has appeared, standing before my eyes,
Saying to me, "Poor girls! what have they done to deserve it,
     Weak and defenseless, a throng thrown on the mercy of men?
You have written two books arming the men with instruction;
     Now let the other side have some help and advice.
Stesichorus, who made, at first, a song against Helen,
     Later extolled her praise, strumming a happier lyre.
If I know you well, as long as you live, you will seek them,
     Girls with a cultured flair; do not be mean to them now."
So she spoke, and bestowed on me the leaves of the myrtle,
     Myrtle, torn from her hair, and a few berries as well.
As I received them I knew, I felt the power of her godhead,
     Air had a purer shine, gloom went away from my heart.
While I am under her spell, O girls, receive my instruction,
     Granted by Venus' grace, granted by warrant of law.

Have your fun while you may, rejoice in the bloom of your spring-
    time,
    Years go by like the waves, rapidly streaming away.
Waves that are once gone by are past the hope of recalling,
    Hours that are once gone by surely will never return.
Take advantage of time; time is a swift-footed glider,
    Nor can the good days to come equal the ones that have fled.
Violets wither and fade; I have seen their color turn ashen,
    Only the stems are left out of the garlands I wore.
There will come a day when you, the excluder of lovers,
    Lie in the lonely night, cold, an old woman, alone.
No one will batter your door or break it with brawls in the night-
    time,
    You will not find in the dawn roses thrown down on the stone.
Most unhappily true—the body is furrowed with wrinkles,
    Shining complexions lose all their bright radiant hues.
Those white hairs which you say you always had, from your girlhood,
    Thicken and multiply fast, covering all of your head.
Serpents put off old age by sloughing their skins with the season,
    Nor do the antlers lost tell the true years of the stag.
All our good things go, and we can do nothing about it,
    Only gather the flower; soon the blossom will fall.
Childbearing shortens your days, the hours of your youthful allot-
    ment—
    Does not the harvest field age from continual yield?
Do as the goddesses did, the Moon with her darling from Latmos,
    Or the rosy Dawn, blushing for Cephalus' love.
Venus mourns, it is true, and never had her Adonis,
    Still, Anchises and Mars gave her a daughter, a son.
Study those ways of theirs, mortals, and from their example
    Do not deny to your men pleasures their eagerness craves.
They will deceive you at last, but what have you lost by it? Nothing.
    Taking a thousand joys, still they take nothing away.

Iron is worn away and flint-stones lessened by usage;
    That part need not fear loss or attrition from time.
Who would forbid us to take light from a light that is offered,
    Who keep account of the waves in the domain of the sea?
So when a woman tells a man, "It doesn't seem proper!"
    What is she doing but waste what her own thirst will require?
I do not want you to be cheap and promiscuous; only
    Fearful of unreal loss: what you are giving you keep.
More of this later on: we still, it seems, are in harbor;
    Here let a fluttering breeze ruffle the swell of the sail.

Cultivation comes first, the proper care of the body—
    From the well-tended vine comes the most exquisite wine.
Beauty's a gift from the gods, too rare for many to boast of:
    Most of you (pardon me, dears) don't have so precious a boon.
So, take pains to improve the endowments nature has given;
    With sufficient neglect, Venus would look like a hag.
If, in the olden days, girls took no care of their persons,
    What did it matter? Of old, men were as crude and uncouth.
If Andromache wore a one-piece garment of burlap,
    What was so strange about that? She was a warrior's spouse.
How would you like to be dressed like the wife of Ajax, in leather,
    Seven layers of hide for your protection from cold?
Simple and rude, those days, but Rome, in our era, is golden,
    Ruler of conquered tribes, holding the wealth of the world.
Look at the Capitol now, and see, in imagination,
    What it used to be, home of a different Jove.
We have a Senate-house worthy of Caesar Augustus,
    Fashioned, in Tatius' reign, out of wattles and clay.
On the Palatine Hill, where Apollo dwells with our princes,
    What did there use to be? Pasture for oxen to browse.
Let others rave about those ancient days; I am happy
    Over the date of my birth: this is the era for me.
Not because we mine the stubborn gold from the mountains,

Not because rare shells come from the farthest of shores,
Not because the hills decrease as we plunder the marble,
Not because sea walls bar raids of the dark-blue sea,
Not for reasons like these, but because our age has developed
Manners, culture and taste, all the old crudities gone.

Do not burden your ears with precious stones from the Indies,
Lifted by dusky men out of the watery green;
Don't stagger under the weight of gold in the seams of your garments—
Too conspicuous wealth frequently puts us to flight.
What we cannot resist is elegance: don't let your hair blow
Wild in the wind, employ just the right touch of the hand.
There are, of course, many styles and pleasing ways of adornment;
Look in your mirror and choose which is most seemly to use.
If your face is long, you should part your hair in the middle;
If your features are round, then let your hair be a crown.
Somebody else might look best with the locks falling over each
shoulder;
That was Apollo's way, god of the resonant lyre.
Still another might try a braid, in the mode of Diana,
Huntress of fugitive game, roaming through woodland and
glade.
Here is a girl who should run her hands through her hair, keep it
fluffy;
There is another whose style calls for the plain and severe.
One might do well with her combs mottled with tortoise-shell markings,
Others do equally well using a wavy design,
But it is foolish to count the acorns that hang on the oak-tree,
Count the bees in the hive, number the fish in the sea,
So I cannot keep track of all the vagaries of fashion,
Every day, so it seems, brings in a different style.
Even neglected hair might prove becoming to many,

Something of yesterday's charm contradicting the comb.
Art may resemble chance, a hint of coincidence in it,
    Art has an off-hand look, sometimes, that multiplies charm.
Think how Iole was seen, in a captured town; in a moment
    Hercules knew, at first sight, she was the woman for him.
Think of the girl from Crete, Ariadne, abandoned on Naxos,
    Lifted in Bacchus' car, cheered by his reveling band.
Nature is fond of you, girls, and generous in her indulgence,
    Offering infinite ways, nice compensations for time.
We poor men, when our hair falls out, are disgustingly naked,
    Bare as the boughs when the wind seizes the wintering leaves.
Women can dye their hair, when it whitens, with Germany's juices,
    Nature improved by art, color surpassing the true.
Women can walk along under a bundle of tresses
    Purchased in any store, new locks replacing the old,
Nor do they blush at the thought; the sales are made in the open,
    Under the Muses' eyes, close to the temple they own.

Now shall I talk about clothes? I do not recommend flounces,
    Do not endorse the wools reddened with Tyrian dye.
When you have such a choice of cheaper and pleasanter colors
    You would be crazy to use only one costly display.
There is the color of sky, light-blue, with no cloud in the heavens,
    There is the hue of the ram, wearing the golden fleece,
There is the color of wave, the hue of the Nereids' raiment,
    There is the saffron glow worn by Aurora at dawn,
All kinds of colors: swans-down, amethyst, emerald, myrtle,
    Almond, chestnut, and rose, yellow of wax, honey-pale—
Colors as many as flowers born from new earth in the springtime,
    When the buds of the vine swell, and old winter has fled,
So many colors, or more, the wool absorbs; choose the right ones—
    Not every color will suit everyone's differing need.
If your complexion is fair, dark-gray is a suitable color;
    Briseis, taken in war, pleased in her gown of dark-gray.

If you are dark, dress in white; such was Andromeda's raiment
    When the envious gods punished her island abode.

Should I warn you to keep the rank goat out of your armpits,
    Warn you to keep your legs free of coarse bristling hair?
No: I am not teaching girls from the rugged Caucasian mountains;
    Those in my school do not drink out of some Mysian mere.
Also, I need not remind you to brush your teeth night and morning,
    Need not remind you your face ought to be washed when you
        rise.
You know what to apply to acquire a brighter complexion—
    Nature's pallidest rose blushes with suitable art.
Art supplies the means for patching an incomplete eyebrow,
    Art, or a beauty-spot, aids cheeks that have never a flaw.
There is nothing amiss in darkening eyes with mascara,
    Ash, or the saffron that comes out of Cilician soil.
I wrote a book about this, *The Art of Beauty*, I called it,
    Not a big book, I must say; still, it took labor and time.
Read it, and find the cure for any defect in your beauty—
    In your interest, you see, mine is a diligent art,
Don't let your lover find the boxes displayed on your dresser,
    Art that dissembles art gives the most happy effect.
Who wants to look at a face so smeared with paint that it's dripping,
    Oozing sluggishly down into the neck of the gown?
I do not think you should use cosmetics offending the nostrils,
    Attar of wool, let us say, drawn from the fleece of the sheep,
Nor do I approve your smearing on marrow in public,
    Using ground pumice stone, cleaning your teeth in plain sight.
Many things add to your charm, but they are unpleasant to look at,
    Many things, ugly to watch, add to your charm if concealed.
Statues that now bear the name of Myron, unwearying artist,
    Once were a lifeless mass, rough and intractable stone.
Gold must be worked into shape before it's a ring for your finger,
    Dresses you put on today once were the grimiest wool.

And that jewel you wear, cameo, brooch, once a nugget—
    Who would have thought it could show Venus, born of the sea?
While you are fixing your face, let us assume you are sleeping,
    Put on the finishing touch privately, out of our sight.
Why do I have to know the cause of your lovely complexion?
    Shut the studio door, don't give the artist away!
There are a great many things that men would be better not know-
       ing:
    Most of your actions offend; keep them away from our sight.
All those statues, those masks, that shine in the theater, golden,
    With the most delicate leaf hiding the crudeness of wood,
Are not allowed to be seen until they are perfectly finished,
    So, you should fashion good looks only while men are away.
Still, they might be allowed to watch you combing and brushing,
    While the wealth of your hair ripples to either side.
Don't, at any such time, shake it out any more than you have to;
    If it should happen to snarl, don't be ill-tempered and cross.
Treat your maid with respect: I hate a woman who scratches,
    Picks on her tiring-maid, jabbing her arms with a pin.
That is the way to make her curse your head, while she tends it,
    Weeping, scared by her blood, hoping you come to no good.
If your hair is not much, be sure the portal is guarded,
    Or be adorned in the fane sacred to women alone.
Once, I remember, I called on a girl who didn't expect me:
    Somehow she managed to get all of her hair upside down!
Let such dishonor as this fall on the Parthian women,
    Be the disgrace of my foes (if I have any of those).
Ugly are hornless bulls, a field without grass is an eyesore,
    So is a tree without leaves, so is a head without hair.

I am not running my school for Semele's sake, nor for Leda's,
    Nor for the girl the white bull carried far over the sea,
Neither for Helen's sake, whom Menelaus demanded,
    Paris wanted to keep, each of them wise in his way.

I teach the rank and file, the pretty ones, also the homely;
    Don't suppose that the good ever outnumber the worse.
Beautiful girls require no help from art, no instruction;
    They have their natural gifts, talents more potent than art.
When the seas are calm, the captain is carefree, unworried;
    When they rise in their wrath, then he appeals to his crew.
Still, the face is rare that has no sign of a blemish;
    Faults of the face or physique call for attempts at disguise.
If you are short, sit down, lest, standing, you seem to be sitting,
    Little as you may be, stretch out full length on your couch.
Even here, if you fear some critic might notice your stature,
    See that a cover is thrown, hide yourself under a spread.
If you're the lanky type, wear somewhat billowy garments,
    Loosely let the robe fall from the shoulders down.
If you're inclined to be pale, wear stripes of scarlet or crimson,
    If you're inclined to be dark, white is an absolute must.
Let an ugly foot hide in a snow-covered sandal;
    If your ankles are thick, don't be unlacing your shoes.
Do your collarbones show? Then wear a clasp at each shoulder.
    Have you a bust too flat? Bandages ought to fix that.
If your fingers are fat, or your fingernails brittle and ugly,
    Watch what you do when you talk; don't wave your hands in the
        air.
Eat a lozenge or two, if you think your breath is offensive,
    If you have something to say, speak from some distance away.
If a tooth is too black, or too large, or the least bit uneven,
    Pay no attention to jokes; laughter might give you away.

Who would believe it? The girls must learn to govern their laughter.
    Even in this respect tact is required, and control.
Do not open the mouth too wide, like a braying she-jackass,
    Show your dimples and teeth, hardly much more than a smile.
Do not shake your sides or slap your thigh in amusement—
    Feminine, that's the idea; giggle or titter, no more.

Some women seem to guffaw as if their faces were bursting,
    Others, for all you can tell, might just as well be in tears.
There is no limit to art: in weeping, you need to be comely,
    Learn how to turn on the tears still keeping proper control.
What about lisping, you ask, or mispronouncing some letters?
    Not a bad trick to acquire; people will label it *Cute!*
Pay close heed to all this, because it is, all of it, useful:
    Posture's important, and poise; walk with a womanly step.
When you go out for the air, remember that people are watching,
    People, men you don't know; you can attract or repel.
Some overdo it, of course, affectedly mincing or swaying,
    Letting the wind blow their clothes, placing their sandals just
        so,
Others go striding along like the sunburnt wife of a farmer,
    Waddle, or take huge strides, jumping a puddle, it seems.
Look! As in everything else, the golden mean is the answer:
    Neither too short nor too long, neither too country nor town.
Keep your snowy arms (if your arms are snowy) uncovered,
    Visible from the left; walk with your shoulders bare.
This is a pleasure to see, and every time that I see it,
    Where the shoulder is bare, I'd put a kiss if I could.
Creatures of ocean, the Sirens sang with melodious voices
    Holding the swiftest ship calmed in its watery course.
Hearing their song, Ulysses fought with the ropes that had bound
        him
    Safe to the mast while the wax deafened the ears of his crew.
Song is a winning art, and girls should certainly learn it;
    Men who are cold to a face yield to a beautiful voice.
Let your repertoire include some popular music,
    Heard in the latest show, foreign songs from the Nile,
Playing the tune yourself, a truly accomplished musician,
    Right hand strumming the strings, left hand holding the lyre.
Orpheus with his lute charmed rocks and trees and wild creatures,
    Even the Furies of Hell had to succumb to his spell.

Amphion played, and the stones of Thebes leaped into position,
    Arion's lyre compelled even the dolphin to hear.
Learn to use both hands on the psalteries of the Phoenicians,
    Making a cheerful noise, bringing all merriment home.

Read some poets, too, Callimachus, and the Coan,
    All that Anacreon wrote, rollicking drinking-songs.
Study Sappho—what girl could set more alluring example?—
    Read Menander, whose plots tell of the wiles of the slave.
You should be able, I hope, to learn some lines of Propertius,
    Poet of our own time, Gallus, Tibullus as well.
Quote from *The Golden Fleece*, that masterpiece written by Varro,
    Don't forget Arms and the Man; Virgil's our greatest and best.
Possibly works of my own may not be considered unworthy,
    Nor will the Lethean stream carry my writings away.
Some one will say: "Be sure to read the songs of our master,
    Ovid, whose elegant art teaches the lore of the heart.
You have three books of the *Loves*, and that is plenty to choose
    from,
    Speaking them soft and low, lines that all lovers should know.
Or, with a practiced voice, read something from one of the *Letters:*
    That was a form of his own; others had left it untried."
Help all this to come true, Apollo and all of the Muses;
    Souls dedicated to song, help me be known in my time!

Who would doubt that a girl should also be clever at dancing,
    When the wine has gone round, gracefully swaying in time?
Actors acquire renown, on our stage, for their movements and ges-
    tures,
    Moving the crowd with their grace, not merely reading their
    lines.
I am almost ashamed to mention some trivial matters,
    Skill at rolling the bones, knowing which player to fade.
Chess is a game to beware: your queen is too apt to be taken,

Castles and knights undone, king in a corner, and—Mate!
Try something simpler, with marbles, or balls in a net or a pocket,
    Possibly tick-tack-toe where you get three in a row.
Make up some games of your own, but always try to play some-
        thing:
    Games are but one of the ways where, in the losing, you win.
It does not mean very much to be clever in all your maneuvers—
    This is much more to the point: keep your temper controlled!
There we can be off guard, betray ourselves, being too eager;
    In our play we reveal what kind of people we are,
Angry, unpleasant to watch, too avaricious for money,
    Quarrelsome, coming to blows, anxious, bewailing our luck,
Telling the others they cheat and filling the air with our grievance,
    Cursing, invoking the gods, tears running out of our eyes.
Don't ever be like this, if you want the men to admire you.
    Nothing is worse in their eyes than a poor loser. Beware!

There are not many games which nature has fashioned for women,
    Nothing like boxing or ball; men have the best of it here.
They can throw the swift spears, or get themselves up in their
        armor,
    They can go riding around, taking the jumps in the field.
You have no place in all this, the ring, or the wrestling arena,
    Nor where the rivers run, cold in the rush of the stream,
But you can walk at your ease by the shadowed arches of Pompey
    When the August sun scorches the roofs of the town,
Visit the Palatine Hill, the temple of laurelled Apollo,—
    His be the praise, whose power saved us from Egypt's design!
Visit the monuments of our leader, his wife, and his sister;
    Look at the naval oak wreathing Agrippa's brow,
Visit the altars of Isis, steaming with incense from Memphis;
    Theaters? All have good seats; choose any one of the three.
Go and look at the games, where the sands are sprinkled with crim-
        son,

Go to the racecourse and watch chariots making the turn.
"Out of sight, out of mind"; and out of mind, out of longing.
What are good looks, unseen? Nothing is gained if you hide.
You may be better at song than Thamyras and all of the Sirens:
If the song is unheard, you might as well be a mute.
Venus would lie in the dark, the deep of the fathomless ocean,
Had not Apelles' art lifted her bright from the foam.
What is the goal of the bards, the great ambition of poets?
Fame is the only reward sought by our arduous toil.
Poets, once on a time, were the care of gods and of monarchs,
On the great choirs of old great were the riches bestowed.
Theirs was a reverend name, theirs was the honor and glory,
Riches and all good gifts fell to the lot of the bard.
Ennius lives in renown, the equal of Scipio, surely,
Ennius, son of the south, born in Calabrian hills.
Now the ivy lies unhonored; his wakeful devotion
Brings the priest of the Muse only a loafer's disgrace.
Yet devotion is good: who would have heard about Homer
If the Iliad's light never came out of his dark?
Who would know Danae now, if her tower had been, always, her
      prison?
She could have perished unknown, nameless as any old crone.
Beautiful girls, a crowd will often serve your advantage:
Step with your little feet frequently over the sill.
Where there are many sheep, the wolf is on watch for a victim,
Where there are many birds, there will the eagle swoop down.
So let a beautiful girl display herself to her public;
Out of the many, she'll find, one may appeal to her mind.
If she is eager to please, let her be a conspicuous pleasure,
Let her, by every device, draw every eye to her charm.
Luck has a part in the game: the hook should forever be dangled;
Where you might least expect there'll be a tug at the line.
Often the hounds in vain harry the glens of the mountains
While the quarry they seek comes, quite by chance, to the snare.

How could Andromeda hope that her tears would find her a lover,
     Bound to the rock in chains, waiting her doom from the sea?
Even tears at the grave of a husband might bring you a new one:
     Weeping and loosened hair heighten a widow's appeal.

Keep away from men who show off their elegant natures,
     Boast of their looks, and arrange every fine hair in its place.
What they are telling you, they have told to girls by the thousand;
     Theirs is a vagabond love, wandering, never at home.
What can a woman do, when a man is smoother than she is,
     Maybe, for all we know, having more men of his own?
This may be hard to believe, but if Troy had listened to Priam,
     She would survive today; take my word, this is true.
Often men grease their way by a false appearance of loving,
     Using the slick approach, seeking your favors by guile.
Don't be fooled by their hair, slicked back and shining with oint-
          ment,
     Nor by the tongue of the belt tightly tucked into the loop,
Don't let a toga deceive you, no matter how silken the texture,
     Don't pay attention to rings worn on more fingers than one.
Possibly, out of them all, the one with the utmost refinement
     Turns out to be just a thief, burning with love for your gown.
"Give me back what is mine!" the girls cry, over and over,
     Making the forum resound—"Give me back what is mine!"
Pleas like these are unheard by Venus and all her attendants
     Where the Appian fount springs near the temple of gold:
There are certainly names that go with a bad reputation;
     Many, I'm sorry to say, hint of a lover deceived.
Learn to look out for yourselves from what you have heard from the
          others:
     When a lover is false, watch it! Don't open your door.
Girls of Athens, beware: don't trust any perjuring Theseus,
     When he swears by the gods—he has sworn falsely before.
Demophoon is as bad, the wanton deceiver of Phyllis;

How can you trust, under oath, men with such records as these?
If they promise you well, why, match them, promise for promise.
   If they live up to their word, give them the joys they deserve.
I think a girl who takes gifts, and then refuses her favors
   Might as well offer a man hemlock and aconite brew.
She would not scruple at all to extinguish the hearth-fires of Vesta,
   Enter a temple and steal sanctified gifts from the shrine.

How I do ramble along! My muse should hold the reins tighter,
   Not let my chariot wheels wobble all over the course.
When a man's paving the way with a letter, in wax, on the tablets,
   Let a maid you can trust bring you the missive he wrote.
Study it, give it some thought; you ought to find out from the phras-
      ing
   Whether he's making it up, whether he writes from the heart.
Answer, after a while: delay is good for a lover—
   Only one bit of advice—don't keep him waiting too long.
Don't be a reckless girl, too quick with a promise, too easy,
   Don't, on the other hand, absolutely refuse.
Let him keep hoping and fearing, and when you send him an answer,
   Give him more cause to hope, lessen his reasons for fear.
Write in conventional terms, with nice and proper expressions;
   Slang or a barbarous style often can frighten a man.
You are not married, I know; you wear no ring on your finger,
   Still, I suppose what you send isn't for everyone's eye,
So have a slave write the words, a boy or a girl doesn't matter,
   Only be sure that the hand goes with a mind you can trust.
I have seen girls turn pale with fright at the risks they have taken,
   Slaves themselves, it would seem, prey of a permanent doubt.
He is a traitorous wretch who would turn such things to advantage,
   Playing with dynamite, fooling with Etnaean fire,
So it is proper and fit to answer cheaters with cheating,
   Self-defense is a right fully protected by law.
Therefore, let your hand learn different methods of writing

(Damn the fellows whose tricks make me give warnings like
    this!)—
Don't send an answer back till you're sure the wax is smoothed over,
    Often one tablet can show traces of different hands.
Always make it appear that your letter is sent to a woman;
    Don't let a gender reveal things that you want to conceal.

Now, if I may, let me turn from trivial matters to greater,
    Spread my billowing sail full to the blast of the gale.
Beauty should take some pains to control wild moments of anger:
    Peace is becoming to men, anger belongs to the brutes.
Features are swollen with rage, and blood makes the arteries blacker,
    Eyes, like Medusa's, or worse, flash with a pestilent fire.
"Go far away from here, flute: you're not worth the trouble you cost
    me,"
    That was Minerva's remark, made to the imaging stream.
If you would look at yourselves, behold your reflection in anger,
    Scarcely a one would admit that was her face in the glass.
Pride is almost as bad, the arrogant, haughty expression;
    Eyes should be gentle and mild, soft for entreating of love.
I hate inordinate pride—will you listen, and trust to an expert?—
    Often a silent face holds all the seeds of contempt.
If he is looking at you, return his gaze, and smile sweetly,
    If he beckons or nods, make some response to his sign.
That is the prologue: the play begins when Cupid, in earnest,
    Draws from his quiver the barb, sharpened to exquisite point.
Also, I hate glum girls: let Ajax have his Tecmessa;
    The life of the party for me; Romans are fun-loving folk.
No Tecmessa for me, and no Andromache, either,
    I would not ask either one "Come to my room after dark!"
I could be wrong, I admit, but, in spite of the fact of their children
    I find it hard to believe they ever slept with a man.
Can you imagine Tecmessa, that dourest and gloomiest woman,
    Murmuring, "Light of my life, Ajax, my darling, my own!"?

Who forbids me to use great things as a model for lesser,
    Who forbids me to bring leadership into my song?
Leadership knows whom to choose, and how to vary assignments,
    Whom to be sent to the troops, whom to the standards and
        stores.
You must also decide which man is best for which purpose,
    Hold an inspection, and set each of us where he belongs.
Let the rich bring gifts; get legal advice from the lawyers;
    Let the eloquent plead, holding the courtroom in thrall.
As for the poets, expect no more from us than our poems—
    We are a chorus trained, more than the others, for love.
We are the heralds who cry the name and fame of our darlings,
    Cynthia, Delia, girls known all over the world;
Who has not heard the name of Lesbia, loved by Catullus?
    Quite a few people inquire who my Corinna may be.
Poets are worshipful men, who never traffic with treason:
    Both our vocation and art keep our characters pure,
Free from the greed for gain, out of the clutch of ambition,
    Scorning the market place, fond of the couch and the shade.
But we are easy to hold, we burn with the strongest of passions,
    Only too well we know loyal devotion in love.
Our native gifts are refined by the gentle art that we practice,
    Our behavior, of course, fits with the ways we pursue.
So, be kind to us, girls, be gracious, always, to poets;
    In them divinity dwells, they are the Muses' own.
There is a god in us, communication with Heaven,
    From the stars of the sky our inspiration comes down.
It is worse than a crime to expect any presents from poets,
    Worse than a crime—but a sin no girl, apparently, fears.
Still, do your best, try hard to mask, for a little, your purpose;
    Even an innocent love shies at the sight of the snare.
No good rider would think of using identical bridles
    On a young colt and a hack hardened by years in the field,
So adapt means to the end: don't try, on a hardened campaigner,

Methods you ought to employ on some young sprout of a boy.
When the raw recruit, brand-new to the barracks of Cupid,
   Prisoner (this he won't know) comes to the door of your room,
Let him know none but you, let him cling to you in devotion—
   High is the hedge that must guard any such tender young bloom.
Share him with nobody else; you will win as long as you hold him
   All by yourself; like a throne, love is a monarch's affair.
But an old soldier will love by degrees, with a gradual wisdom,
   He will be patient and bear what no recruit would endure.
He will not break down your doors, nor burn them in desperate passion,
   He will not scratch with his nails, clawing your delicate cheek,
He will not rip off his clothes nor tear your dress from your shoulder,
   He will not make you weep, yanking out handfuls of hair.
Those are the acts of boys, the young, the lovesick, the foolish;
   Your old campaigner endures wounds with composure of mind.
He will burn with slow fire, like a torch that smoulders in damp air,
   Like the green timber cut down not long ago on the hills.
His is a surer love; the other's is brief, but more fruitful:
   Pluck the fruit and be quick—only too soon it is gone.

Might as well open the gates, admit the foe, in our treason,
   In our faithlessness keep faith, in our renegade way.
Gifts too easily made encourage no permanent passion—
   Mix in a little rebuff, once in a while, with your fun.
Let him lie on the stone, complain that the door is too cruel,
   Let him be meek as a mouse, then let him threaten and rave.
Sweetness we cannot stand: refresh us with juice that is bitter.
   Often a boat goes down sunk by a favoring wind.
That is what keeps some wives from being loved by their husbands:
   It's all too easy for him, coming whenever he will.
Put a door in his way, and have a doorkeeper tell him
   "No admittance: keep out!"—then he will burn with desire.
Put your blunt swords down, and take up deadlier weapons,

Turn them on me (I suppose that's what I'll get for my pains).
When he falls into the snare, your lover, just recently captured,
    Ought to be made to feel he is the only one there.
Later on, let him know you go to bed with a rival:
    Fail in this, you will find ardor beginning to wane.
Your true thoroughbred, when the starting gate is thrown open,
    Runs his best race in a field where he must come from behind.
Fires that are burning low are fanned into flame by an outrage.
    Look at me! I ought to know; I can love only when wronged.
Still, let the cause of the grief be not unduly apparent,
    Let him worry, suspect more than he actually knows.
It will arouse him to hear of a slave (whom you may have invented)
    Glumly on guard, or the dour stare of a husband, that pest.
Pleasure too safely enjoyed is that much less of a pleasure:
    Though you are perfectly free, freer than Thais, act scared.
When you might let him in by the door, let him in by a window,
    Let your features assume every expression of fright,
Have your maid rush in (she will have to be clever about it)
    Crying, "My God, we're sunk!"; hide the poor frightened young
        man.
Yet, in spite of the fear, you must give him some genuine pleasure;
    Don't let him get the idea nights in your house aren't worth
        while.

I was about to omit the art of deceiving a husband,
    Fooling a vigilant guard, crafty though either might be.
Let the bride honor, obey, pay proper respect to her husband,
    That is only correct; decency says so, and law.
But why should you, set free, and not too long ago, either,
    By the decree of the court, have to be kept like a bride?
Listen to me, and learn; though your watchers are there by the hun-
        dred,
    If you will take my advice, you can get rid of them all.
How can they interfere or stop you from writing a letter?

What is a bathroom for? Tell them you have to go there.
    Haven't you any close friend who knows how to carry a tablet
        Under her arm, or perhaps tucked in the fold of a gown?
Isn't she able to hide a note in the top of her stocking,
        Or, if that's apt to be found, in the instep of a shoe?
Is her guardian on to such tricks?—let her offer herself as a tablet,
        Carry, in code, on her back, letters in lipstick of red.
For your invisible ink, use milk: it will show when you heat it;
        Write with a stem of wet flax—no one will ever suspect.
Danae's father supposed he was careful in guarding his daughter;
        He was a grandfather soon, proving his vigilance vain.
What can a guardian do, with theaters all through the city?
        What can a guardian do when a girl goes to the track?
What can he do when she kneels to offer her homage to Isis?
        That is a place where no man ever has freedom to go.
There are more temples than one from which male eyes are forbid-
    den,
        Where the Good Goddess allows only her servants to come.
What can a guardian do but sit and look at her clothing
        When a girl goes to the baths, finding her games and her fun?
What is the use? She must go to take care of a friend, in a sickroom;
        Then her friend's perfectly well, leaving her half of the bed.
What can be done when the town is full of experienced locksmiths,
        When it's not only the door letting you enter at will?
Even the cheapest wine from Spain will befuddle a guardian;
        Drugs are effective as well, working with opiate spell.
He can be put to sleep if you send your maid to seduce him,
        Keeping him by her side, joined in delightful delay.
Why do I waste so much time with all this instruction in detail?
        There is an easier way; it won't take much of a bribe.
Take my word for it, bribes can buy both men and immortals;
        Jupiter, even, is won if you bring gifts to his shrine.
Fools will brag about bribes, but what can be done with a wise man?
        Bribe him. He'll take the bribe; furthermore, he will keep still.

But remember one thing—you're paying for permanent service,
    Yours is a long-term lease; see that the bribe is enough.
I recall making complaints about friends who were not to be trusted:
    This, you can be very sure, happens not only with men.
Don't trust the other girls: they'll steal your man in a second,
    Hunters, that's what they are, having no conscience at all.
Also, beware of the friend who has a spare room for your lover.
    I know how that works out; I've been there many a time.
One final word of advice: don't let your maid be too pretty—
    Often a maid will do all you would like to, and more.

I must be out of my mind! Here I go, wholly defenseless,
    Into the enemy's camp, giving my secrets away.
Even a bird has more sense than to tell where the fowler may find it,
    Deer do not teach the pack where the hounds are to run.
Well, never mind: I began, and so I might as well finish,
    Keeping the promise I made, guiding the sword to my heart.
Make us believe we are loved, and that is an easy assignment;
    What we desire we shall find, out of the reach of our doubt.
So, let a woman look at a man with her sweetest affection,
    Sigh from the depths of her heart, ask why he got there so late,
Let her throw in a few tears, pretend to be hurt by a rival,
    Rake his face with her nails—that will convince him, for sure.
Satisfied, sure of himself, he will turn to expressions of pity,
    Saying, "The poor little thing! Isn't she wild about me?"
If he is smart in his dress, when he looks at himself in a mirror,
    He will be prone to believe goddesses swoon at the sight.
No matter what he may do, be sure not to let it disturb you;
    Hearing about some one else, don't you go out of your mind!
Don't be too quick to believe the worst: the story of Procris
    Warns you what damage is done if you are jealous too soon.

Near the blue hills of Hymettus, whose flowers are always in blos-
    som,

173

There is a sacred spring, turf eternally green.
Trees of no great height make a grove, and a carpet of berries
    Crimsons the grass: you can find rosemary, myrtle, and bay.
Thick-leaved boxwood is there, and the tamarisks, fragile and sway-
    ing,
    Tender lucerne and the pine, tended with delicate care.
Breezes come wandering there, and the air is always in motion,
    Leaves rustle over your head, the tips of the grasses bend.
This was a resting place for Cephalus, wearied from hunting,
    On this green ground he would lie, leaving his hounds and his
    train.
Here he would call to the breeze, "Come, wandering Aura, refresh
    me;
    Come to my arms and my heart, cooling the heat of my fire."
Somebody, hearing the words, and more than a little officious,
    Thought his wife should be told: who was this Aura he called?
Only the name of the breeze, but Procris believed her a rival,
    Fainted away in her grief, terror-stricken and dumb,
Turned as pale as the leaves that are left on the grapevine in au-
    tumn,
    Pale as the whitening grain when the first hoarfrost has come,
Or as ripe quinces that bend the hanging boughs in the summer,
    Pale as the cornel-fruit, not yet fully mature.
When she revived, straightway she tore the gown from her bosom,
    Scratched at her innocent cheeks, loosened her hair to the
    wind,
Stormed through the streets in a rage, as wild as any Bacchante,
    Under the spell of the god, called by the flutes and the drum.
When she was almost there, she left her companions behind her,
    Quiet, suspicious, and brave, stealthily entered the grove.
What could your feeling have been when you hid yourself there in
    the thicket,
    Procris, whose sensitive heart burned with unquenchable fire?

You must have thought she would come, whoever she might be,
　　that Aura,
　　Come for your eyes to behold, caught in the act of her shame.
Now she is sorry she came, would rather not prove he is guilty,
　　Now she is glad; her love shifts with each beat of her heart.
There was that name, and this place, and the story to make her be-
　　lieve it,
　　Also, the fears of the mind make apprehension seem true.
She can see where the grass has been flattened by somebody's lying,
　　She can see, and her heart leaps with excitement and fear.
It was noontime by now, the balance of morning and evening,
　　Now the tall of the day shortened the bodiless shade.
Cephalus came from the woods: he was there, the son of Cyllene,
　　Flushed from the chase, and his hands seeking the cool of the
　　spring.
Procris was very still, and very worried, and watched him,
　　Heard him call, as he lay, "Fan me, dear Aura, and come!"
Then she understood, and the error was almost a pleasure,
　　Color came back to her cheeks, reason returned to her mind.
Rising, she started to break through the leaves between her and her
　　loved one,
　　Eagerly parted the boughs, a girl on her way to a man.
Cephalus, hearing the sound, suspected a beast in the thicket,
　　Ready again for the hunt, poising the spear in his hand.
What are you doing, you fool? 'Tis no wild creature you aim at,
　　Checking your aim, too late: the quarry was only a girl.
"Woe, alas!" she cried, "my heart, one way or another,
　　Always receives the wound, Cephalus causes my hurt.
Dying before my time, I can make no complaint of a rival:
　　Cover me lightly, earth, in my commitment to doom.
Now my spirit goes to the breeze whose name I suspected;
　　Let the hand I love close my wearying eyes!"
Sadly, and all in vain, he lifts his wife to his bosom,

Holds her close as he can, washes the wound with his tears,
But her spirit goes, deserting the credulous body,
Slowly; the lips of the man take the last breath of his love.

Let us get back to our work: we must come to the heart of the
matter,
So that my weary keel reaches the haven at last.
You are anxiously waiting for me to escort you to parties,
In this area, too, willing to heed my advice.
When the lamps have been lit, make a graceful, and leisurely, en-
trance;
All that has happened before seems to build up for your charm.
You may be rather plain, but the shadows will help you conceal it,
So, to those who are tight, you will look just about right.
Daintiness matters: be sure to help yourself with your fingers
In the most ladylike way; don't feed your face with a paw.
Don't just pick at your food, as if you had had a big dinner;
Don't, on the other hand, gobble as much as you can.
Even a Helen would seem repulsive, a horrible creature,
Taking too much at a meal, stuffing herself to the ears.
Drinking is more *à propos*, and better becoming a woman;
Bacchus and Venus' son make a convivial team.
Don't let it go to your head: as long as you're not seeing double,
You should be able to walk, keeping control of your mind.
Nothing is worse to behold than a woman, passed out: how disgust-
ing!
She has deserved to be laid in the most sodden embrace.
Don't go falling asleep when the table is cleared; in your slumber
Things can happen that you, waking, would deem a disgrace.

In our last lesson we deal with matters peculiarly secret;
Venus reminds us that here lies her most intimate care.
What a girl ought to know is herself, adapting her method,

Taking advantage of ways nature equips her to use.
Lie on your back, if your face and all of your features are pretty;
    If your posterior's cute, better be seen from behind.
Milanion used to bear Atalanta's legs on his shoulders;
    If you have beautiful legs, let them be lifted like hers.
Little girls do all right if they sit on top, riding horseback;
    Hector's Andromache knew she could not do this: too tall!
Press the couch with your knees and bend your neck backward a
        little,
    If your view, full-length, seems what a lover should crave.
If the breasts and the thighs are youthful and lovely to look at,
    Let the man stand and the girl lie on a slant on the bed.
Let your hair come down, in the Laodamian fashion:
    If your belly is lined, better be seen from behind.
There are a thousand ways: a simple one, never too tiring,
    Is to lie on your back, turning a bit to the right.
My Muse can give you the truth, more truth than Apollo or Am-
        mon;
    Take it from me, what I know took many lessons to learn.
Let the woman feel the act of love to her marrow,
    Let the performance bring equal delight to the two.
Coax and flatter and tease, with inarticulate murmurs,
    Even with sexual words, in the excitement of play,
And if nature, alas! denies you the final sensation
    Cry out as if you had come, do your best to pretend.
Really, I pity the girl whose place, let us say, cannot give her
    Pleasure it gives to the man, pleasure she ought to enjoy.
So, if you have to pretend, be sure the pretense is effective,
    Do your best to convince, prove it by rolling your eyes,
Prove by your motions, your moans, your sighs, what a pleasure it
        gives you.
    Ah, what a shame! That part has its own intimate signs.
After the joys of love, a girl who will ask for a present
    Surely is wasting her time: that's not a nice thing to do.

Don't let the light pour in, with all of the windows wide open—
    It is more fitting to keep much of your body concealed.

So our sport has an end: our swans are tired of their harness:
    Time for their labors to rest, time to step down from our car.
As the young men did, now let the girls, my disciples,
    Write on the votive spoil, "Ovid showed us the way."

THE
REMEDIES
FOR
LOVE

Love read the name of this book before I had written a sentence.
  "Wars," he remarked, "I can see clearly are waiting for me."
"O Cupid," I said in reply, "don't think me a criminal poet;
  I have so often borne standards of yours to the wars.
I am no Diomede, who wounded your beautiful mother,
  Sending her back to the skies, drawn by the horses of Mars.
Some young men, sometimes, are cold; I have been, always, a lover:
  What am I doing now? Well may you ask—I'm in love.
Often I taught folks the arts, the science, of winning you over;
  What was an impulse at first now is a system, full-grown.
I am no traitor, dear boy, no renegade, turncoat, deserter,
  Nor does my newer Muse ravel the work of the old.
Let all men who find that love is a pleasure, keep loving,
  Burn with a happy fire, sail on a favoring wind,
But if any one grieves, is oppressed by the yoke of a tyrant,
  Let him not perish, but feel comfort my art can convey.
Why has some poor wretch made use of a rope for his collar,
  Hanging himself from a beam, pitiful victim of love?
Why has another one pierced his heart with a desperate sword-
    thrust?
  Cupid, lover of peace, you are a killer, I claim.

If a man is to die, unless he recovers from loving,
    Let him recover, in time; you will be guiltless of crime.
You are a boy; at your age nothing but play is becoming;
    Play, then; gentle and mild be the dominion you hold.
Certainly you could have used the deadliest shafts in your battles,
    But the arrows you aim never should redden with blood.
Let your stepfather fight with the sword and the lance and the
        spear-point,
    Let him victorious go, stained with the blood of the foe.
Cherish your mother's arts, whereby we are all of us safer,
    Cherish those arts whereby no other mother can grieve.
Let lovers batter the doors, break through in their brawling at
        night-time,
    Let the posts of the doors hide under garlands of flowers,
Make the boys and the girls keep getting together in secret,
    Furnish the words to deceive husbands, whatever their guile.
Let the lover, shut out, curse at the door that prevents him,
    Let him, sad on the step, sing his pathetic refrain.
Be content with these tears, without resorting to murder:
    Yours is a torch, as we know, not for the funeral pyre."
So I reproved him, and Love, all golden, gave me an answer,
    Moving his jewelled wings—"Finish the work you propose."

So now listen to me, young men who have been so deluded,
    Whom, for all of your pains, love has completely betrayed.
I have taught you to love—do you want to know how to recover?
    Mine is the hand that will bring wounds, and the cure for the
        wound.
Earth, in her way, brings forth the poisonous herbs and the healing;
    Often the nettle is found close by the side of the rose.
Telephus, Hercules' son, was hurt by the spear of Achilles,
    Yet that very spear brought the relief of his pain.
(What I am saying applies to both of the parties contending—
    Girls as well as the men draw their arms from my store.)

Something I say may not pertain to your needs of the moment;
  Nevertheless, pay heed: some day it might be of use.
It is a worth-while art, to extinguish the fires of your ardor,
  Never to let the heart be its own piteous slave.
Phyllis would still be alive if she had listened to Ovid,
  Never have taken her nine desperate ways to the sea,
Nor would Dido, in death, have seen from the top of her watch-
      towers,
  Trojan ships in their flight, spreading their sails to the wind.
Nor would Medea have slain her sons in her anger and vengeance,
  Punishing Jason's crime, killing the children she bore.
Tereus, heeding my art, however he loved Philomela,
  Need not have taken to rape, need not have changed to a bird.
Give me Pasiphae: she will take no bull for her lover;
  Give me Phaedra: her love need not become a disgrace.
Give me Paris, and Helen will never desert Menelaus,
  Nor will the walls of Troy ever be razed for her doom.
What if the daughter of Nisus had read the books I have written?
  Still his purple lock would have remained on his head.
Under my guidance, men, restrain your ruinous passions;
  Under my guidance sail safely, both captain and crew.
When you were learning to love, you certainly had to read Ovid:
  Ovid's the writer to read; there is no difference now.
I am your public defender, emancipator and healer:
  Call it a rod or a wand, mine is the touch that sets free.
As I begin my work, Apollo, lord of the laurel,
  Lord of healing and song, come with your blessing and aid.

While you still have a chance, and your heart is moved, but not
      deeply,
  If you're uncertain at all, never step over the sill.
Crush, before they are grown, the swelling seeds of your passion,
  Let your spirited steed never get into full stride.
What is delayed grows strong: delay is the agent, maturing

Purple grapes on the vine, yellowing wheat in the ear.
What was it once, that tree with its great shade over the strollers?
    Sapling, or less, which one hand might have pulled out of the
        ground.
Now it is grown to full height, and arches over with shadow,
    Firm in its root, immense, come to the full of its bloom.
Watch, with circumspect mind, what kind of a thing you are lov-
        ing:
    Get your neck from the yoke, if you suspect it will gall.
Fight the disease at the start, for once the symptoms develop
    Medicine comes too late, losing effect from delay.
So be as prompt as you can, don't put things off till tomorrow;
    If you're not ready today, when are you going to start?
Love is good at excuses, and love is fed by delaying;
    If you aspire to be free, there is no time like today.
You do not often see rivers run deep at their sources,
    Most of them come to full flood gathering strength as they
    flow.
Myrrha, quicker to sense the criminal urge of her nature,
    Might have been spared her disgrace, turned to the sorrowful
    tree,
I have seen a wound that might have been healed when inflicted
    Fester with long delay, aggravated by time.
But because we delight in plucking the blossoms of Venus
    Always we say to ourselves: "Tomorrow will be just the same."
Meanwhile the devious flame creeps subtly into our vitals,
    Meanwhile the evil tree thrives with the roots going deep.
Yet if the chance is lost, if no first aid can be given,
    If the disease of love, chronic, possesses the heart,
We have a serious case, but, though I am called to the patient
    All too late for his good, still we must never despair.
Philoctetes, of course, should have put the knife to the tissue,
    Cut the infection away, lone on the Lemnian isle,

Yet he was healed, we believe, as the years went by, and his weap-
　　ons,
　　　Hercules' arrow and bow, ended both Troy and the war.
I, who was rushing along, to cure your disease at its onset,
　　　Bring to you, late and slow, what medication I can.
Either put out the fire, when you can, at its very beginning,
　　　Or, if you must, stand aside, watching it burn itself out.
While its madness drives on, retreat from the drive of that madness,
　　　Whose impetuous rush sweeps opposition away.
Foolish the swimmer who tries to struggle against the current
　　　When he could slant his course, easing his progress down
　　　　stream.
Oh, I know, I know: the spirit, at first, is impatient,
　　　Hates and refuses advice, sneers at the counselling word.
So I bide my time, until the patient is ready,
　　　Willing to hear the truth, letting me bandage the wound.
Who but a fool would attempt to stop a mother from grieving
　　　Over the tomb of her son? That is no time for advice.
When she has shed her tears, and her season of anguish is waning,
　　　Then is the time to bring words to alleviate pain.
Timing itself is an art, almost a department of healing:
　　　Wine may be sometimes a risk, sometimes a positive cure.
If you attack a disease, be sure the time is propitious:
　　　Some inflammations increase if you repress them too soon.

So, when I find you at last submissive, willing to listen,
　　　Take my advice. Point one—shun all leisurely ways.
Idleness tempts you to love, and idleness watches its captives,
　　　Idleness feeds on its prey, makes the infection delight.
Toss your leisure away, and you've broken the arrows of Cupid,
　　　Toss your leisure away, his torch is extinguished and scorned.
As the plane-trees rejoice in wine, or the poplars in water,
　　　As the reeds by the pool cherish the watery cool,

So does Venus delight in idleness: keep yourself busy
    If you would drive her away; if you are busy, you're safe.
Listlessness, too much sleep with no alarm clock to wake you,
    Gambling, getting your wits over-befuddled with wine,
These can exhaust the nerves and leave the spirit defenseless,
    Where the way is prepared, Love comes stealthily in.
Cupid, pursuer of loafers, despises those who are active;
    Give to your idle mind work that requires to be done.
There are the courts of the law, and friends who need a defender—
    In the white garb of the town there is distinguished renown.
Or go off to the wars, assume the duties of service,
    Spend your youth in the field where no frivolity reigns.
Look, the Parthian host in retreat, new cause of our triumph,
    See on their plains by now Caesar's victorious arms.
Cupid and Parthians both favor the arrow as weapon;
    Triumph over them both, double the trophies brought home.
Soon as Venus was hurt with a wound from Diomed's spear-point
    She retired from the field, summoning Mars to the fray.
Why did Aegisthus succumb to that adulterous passion?
    That is no trouble at all—he had nothing to do.
Others were fighting at Troy in the drawn-out years of the conflict,
    All of Greece had been drained, all of her strength oversea,
There were no wars to be waged, or any battles, in Argos,
    There were no cases in court, nothing for pleaders to do,
So he did what he could: loving was better than nothing—
    That is how Cupid sneaks in, turning the sentence around.

Also, the mind can be charmed by the care of a place in the coun-
    try:
    If you are farming, my boy, you won't have time for much else.
Make the tamed bulls learn to bend to the yoke and the harness,
    So that the curve of the plough wounds the refractory ground;
Bury the seeds in the soil, prepare for the yield of the harvest;
    Watch the branches bend, heavy with fruit on the tree,

Look at the flowing streams, and hear their melodious murmur,
    Look at the sheep as they graze over the green of the field.
See how the goats climb rocks, up the precipitous ledges,
    Soon to bring home for their kids udders distended and full.
On his uneven pipe the shepherd makes himself music,
    While his companion attends—man's best friend is his dog.
Somewhere, farther off, the woodland echoes the lowing
    While a mother cow calls for her calf to come home.
What of the sound of the bees, fleeing the smoke of the torches,
    So that the baskets' withes hold the curve of the comb?
Autumn brings apples, and summer is beautiful over the grainfields,
    Spring has blossoms to give, winter is lightened by fire.
Everything in due time for the man who lives in the country,
    Plucking the ripened grape, treading the crimsoning juice,
Everything in due time, harrowing, reaping and binding,
    Planting in watered ground, guiding the rivulet's run,
Grafting, slip to bough, in the fertile bond of adoption,
    So that the tree stands tall, covered with leaves not its own.
Once these pleasures begin to soothe the mind and the spirit,
    Love, on ridiculous wing, flutters defeated away.
Or have a try at the hunt: Venus has often retreated,
    Often been routed in shame, when Diana appears.
Take your pack of hounds, pursue the skittering rabbit,
    Spread the mesh of the nets high on the leaf-covered ridge,
Start the timid deer, or strike the boar with your spear-point—
    Sleep will receive you at night, not the desire for a girl.
Less exciting, but fun, are sports like fishing and fowling,
    Taking your birds with the net, catching your fish on the line.
This way or that, never mind—one way is as good as another
    So you keep fooling yourself, subtly unlearning to love.
Strong though your chains may be, determined to hold you forever,
    Break them, go far away, fare to the ends of the world.
You will cry out for your loss, bewailing the name of your loved
    one,

Often your foot will stop right in the midst of the road,
If you're reluctant to go, be more determined on going:
    Keep on your way; if your feet dawdle, see to it they run.
No use praying for rain, or thinking it might be the Sabbath—
    Any ill-omened day is better to travel than stay.
Don't ask how far you have gone, or what remains of the journey,
    Don't be contriving delays keeping you nearer at hand,
Don't count the hours and the days, and don't look back at the city,
    Keep on going; escape lies in the Parthian flight.

Some one may call my advice cruel and hard: I admit it.
    Still, if you want to be well, therapy must be endured.
When I was sick myself, I often drank down bitter tonics,
    Often denied myself food, fighting the urge of my will.
For your bodily health, you submit to the steel and endure it,
    Nor will the water's cool slake your feverish thirst.
So, for your mental health, is any treatment too drastic?
    Ailments of mind demand more than placebos to cure.
Strait is the gate, I know, an ordeal and a terrible trial,
    Once a beginning is made, then it is easy to bear.
Have you not seen how the yoke first galls the necks of the oxen,
    How the new cinch at first troubles the swift-footed steed?
Possibly leaving your home will be more than a little bit irksome:
    Nevertheless, you will go; then you will want to return,
Not so much to your home, for all your pathetic excuses,
    No, you will want to be back in the arms of a girl.
Once you have really gone, you will find there are hundreds of comforts,
    Comrades and country scenes, even the reach of the road.
Do not think it enough to depart; you also must linger,
    Stay till the fire burns low, stay till the ashes are cool.
If you return too soon, before your mind has recovered,
    Love will attack you again, fierce with implacable arms.

Absence will do you no good if you come back thirsty and greedy,
 All of the time you have spent prove a delusion and snare.

Now, if anyone thinks that Haemonian simples can help him,
 Magic effect his cure, let him take care of himself.
That is an obsolete way, that kind of witchcraft: Apollo
 Proffers me innocent aid, healing, the gift of the song.
Under my guidance no shade will stalk by night in the graveyard,
 No aged sorceress cleave earth with her infamous spell,
No standing wheat will shift from one man's field to another's,
 Nor will the orb of the sun suddenly fade and grow pale,
Tiber will flow to the sea in Tiber's usual fashion,
 After her custom the moon ride in her snow-white car.
No enamored hearts will ever be cured by enchantments,
 Nor is the rout of love ordered by sulphurous fumes.
How were the herbs of Thrace of any avail to Medea?
 How could Circe keep Ithacan vessels from home?
Try as she would, she failed to keep Ulysses from leaving;
 Wily, he spread his sail full to the wind of his flight.
Try as she would, she failed to keep the flame from her marrow,
 Deep in her heart it burned, stubborn and obdurate love.
Men she could change into beasts, but the laws of her passionate
  nature—
 Those she could not change, helpless against her desire.
"I do not pray any more," she told him, eager for sailing,
 "As I remember I prayed, wanting you anxious to be
Husband of mine, and I seemed a worthy wife for Ulysses,
 Goddess in my own right, child of the powerful Sun.
What I do pray for is this—delay; give me time as a present!
 How could I ask for less? That is the sum of my prayer.
See how the waters rage and roar; you ought to be fearful.
 Wait for a better wind; that will not be very long.
What is the cause of your flight? Here no new Troy is arising,

No one calls to the wars old companions in arms.
Here is love and peace (except that in peace I am wounded),
    All this land will be under your lordship and rule."
That was what Circe said—Ulysses loosened his cable;
    Winds that filled his sail carried her words to—nowhere.
Circe, burning, resorts to the arts whose practice she knows well;
    Circe's passion is healed by no magical charm.

So, whoever you are who come to me for your healing,
    Have no faith in spells, let the enchantments alone.
If some powerful cause is keeping you here in the city,
    Take the prescription I give all who must stay in the town:
He can free himself best who has broken the shackles that bind
    him,
    Shaken the hurt from his heart, forever and ever, amen.
I would be greatly surprised to find a man of such will power;
    If I did, I would say, "He does not need my advice!"
Come to me if you love and want to be rid of your loving,
    Want to, and yet cannot; scholar, be taught in my school!
Try to remember her deeds, her wicked, wanton behavior,
    Itemize, if you can, all she has cost you to date.
"She has this, she has that, she is never content with her booty,
    Even my household gods have to be mortgaged or sold!
She has sworn me true, and played me false in the swearing.
    How many times I have spent nights on the stone at her door!
Others she loves, but me—? She is much too nice to be bothered.
    Any old peddler can have nights she refuses to me."
Let such memories ret your feelings in gall and in wormwood,
    Never forget to sow seeds of contempt in your mind.
What you need to acquire is eloquence, denunciation,
    Vigorous, passionate: well—suffer enough, you will learn.
Not long ago a girl, or should I say an obsession,
    Troubled my peace of mind—what an appalling affair!
Doctor Ovid was sick, and applying his own medication,

I was the doctor, and sick, really a desperate case.
One thing did me some good, a most repetitious insistence
　　On every one of her faults; that brought effective relief.
I would say, "Look at her legs; did you ever see any that ugly?"
　　(That was a lie; her legs really weren't ugly at all.)
"What a runt!" (She was tall.) "How much she demands of a
　　　lover!"
　　　(That had a trace of the truth; that, mostly, helped me to
　　　hate.)
Virtue and vice, evil and good, are siblings, or next-door neighbors,
　　Easy to make mistakes, hard to tell them apart.
When you possibly can, fool yourself, ever so little,
　　Call those attractions of hers defects, or possibly worse.
If she has full round breasts, call her *fat as a pig*; if she's slender,
　　Thin as a rail; if she's dark, *black as the ace of spades*.
If she has city ways, label her *stuck-up* and *bitchy*;
　　If she is simple and good, call her *a hick from the farm*.
Whatever talent she lacks, coax and cajole her to use it:
　　If she hasn't a voice, try to persuade her to sing;
If she trips over her feet, make her dance; if her accent's atrocious,
　　Get her to talk; all thumbs?—call for the zither or lyre.
If she waddles or limps, be sure to take her out walking;
　　If she has bulging breasts, don't let her wear a brassière.
If her teeth aren't too straight, tell her a comical story;
　　Make it a sorrowful tale if she has watery eyes.
Sometimes it works very well to surprise her early some morning,
　　Hardly expecting a call, when she's not fixed for the day.
All of us let ourselves be fooled by a woman's adornments,
　　Jewels and gold; we see more than there is to the girl.
Sometimes I wonder where, in the midst of all this abundance,
　　Lies the essence of love, under the shield and disguise.
So, come unforeseen: safe, you will catch her defenseless,
　　Sorry to see and be seen, victim and failure and fraud.
(Still, it is not too safe to trust this prescription too blindly;

Beauty, artless, naïve, often has power to deceive.)
Go take a look some time when she's smearing her face with cos-
    metics—
    Don't let a little thing like decency stand in your way—
You will find boxes and things, a thousand different colors,
    Also lotions and such, dripping all over her chest.
Drugs like these smell worse than the tables the Harpies polluted,
    Giving me, more than once, more than an impulse to retch.

As for the act of love—keep passion away altogether;
    Much I might say to you now I am ashamed to put down.
Read between the lines: some people, I know, are complaining,
    Calling my books obscene, saying my Muse is a whore.
Just as long as I please, as I do, and the world is my public,
    Let these nobodies gain what satisfaction they can.
Envy attacks the great, even the genius of Homer;
    Zoilus, whoever he was, battened on Homer's renown.
Impious tongues have dared to slander the measures of Virgil
    Under whose guidance Troy brought her religion to Rome.
Envy attacks the heights, as winds sweep over the summit,
    As the bolts of Jove find the conspicuous mark.
Well, whoever you are, in case my license offends you,
    Learn at least this much—manner must go with the theme.
Wars and the deeds of the brave require the measures of Homer;
    How could hexameter verse deal with the pleasures of love?
When the buskin is on, the actor is solemn and tragic,
    For his commoner scenes, the sock is the symbol to wear.
Elegy, charming and gay, sings of the boy with the quiver,
    Elegy plays at her whim in no responsible mood.
Not for Callimachus' muse are the deeds of mighty Achilles
    Nor should Cydippe's ruse call for a Homer to tell.
Cast for Andromache's role a Thais: who could endure it?
    Nor should Andromache read Thais's wantoner lines.
Thais is in my art, and my license goes where it pleases.

I wear no frightening mask; Thais is in my art.
If my Muse is accused of being a little bit funny,
    I would plead guilty and win; throw the case out of court!
Envy, swell up and burst! My name is distinguished already;
    It will be greater yet, keeping the pace it has set.
Envy, don't burst too soon! As long as I live, I shall give you
    More to be sorry about; I have so much I can sing.
Oh, it's delightful to sing, for the joy as well as the honor—
    Watch my Bucephalus fly, hardly around the first turn!
Elegy owes me as much, and would be the first to admit it,
    As the Epic muse owes to Virgilian art.

That should be more than enough by way of an answer to Envy.
    Poet, back to your work; run the appropriate track!
Now, where were we? Oh yes—the right true business of manhood,
    When the hour of the night calls to the promised delight.
Lest you enjoy it too much, if you take it with all of your vigor,
    I would suggest that you try someone a little before.
Go to some other girl for the first excitement and pleasure,
    That which follows will seem, maybe, a bit of a bore.
Pleasure coming slow is the best, the warmth in the chillness,
    Shade in the glare of the sun, water that quenches the thirst.
This I should not say, but I will: adopt a position
    Awkward for her and for you, hardly becoming or fit.
This is no trouble at all; few women will ever acknowledge
    There is a better way; this they can never admit.
Open the windows wide, all of them, draw back the curtains,
    Let the light make clear parts that are ugly to see.
When you have come to the end, and all the pleasure is over,
    When the body and mind both are exhausted and spent,
While you are bored, and you wish you never had touched any
        woman,
    While you haven't the least impulse to touch one again,
Then note down in your mind her every blemish of body,

Keep your eyes on her faults, memorize every defect.
Possibly some one will say, and be right, that they're really quite
    small ones;
    Still, the little things count; all of them come to your aid.
How big an asp does it take to kill an ox or a bullock?
    Often the least of the hounds holds at bay the wild boar.
Safety in numbers!—fight on, add up the sum of my precepts;
    Pile up the numerous grains, mountains of counsel arise.
But, since the ways we react seem to differ as much as our features,
    Do not trust me too far; use your own judgment at times.
Something that could, perhaps, give no offense to your feelings
    Might seem a monstrous crime, viewed by another man's eyes.
One man, just at the point, when he looked at those parts gaping
    open,
    Faltered and failed, desire fading like yesterday's rose.
Somebody else, when the girl arose from the business of loving,
    Noticed, disgusted, the stains left on the sheets of the bed.
You do not really care, if matters like these can affect you;
    Feeble, indeed, is the torch kindling the flame in your hearts.
One fine day that Boy will loose his deadlier arrows,
    Then, a wounded throng, you will be looking for aid.
What of the man who lay hid, and watched while the girl was
    performing
    Rites that custom forbids masculine eyes to behold?
God forbid that I should offer my patients such counsel!
    Though it might possibly help, better to leave it alone.
This I do recommend: that you have a couple of sweethearts.
    If you can manage more, so much the better for you.
When the distracted mind swings off in either direction,
    Then the passion is less, trouble divided by two.
Channels can make great floods become the tiniest streamlets;
    Raging fires die down, soon as the fuel is split.
No one anchor holds the pitchy keels in the roadstead,
    No one hook is enough, dropped in the run of the wave.

194

He who long ago found double comfort to cheer him
  Long ago became victor, enthroned in the heights.
You, however, who made the mistake of having one only,
  Now must attempt to find a second string for your bow.
Minos' love for his queen died out in his passion for Procris,
  Nor could Oenone keep Paris from Helen's embrace.
Tereus, Philomel, and Procris—but why should I bore you
  Counting the number of times love was succeded by love?
Grief for a son is less in the heart, if his brothers survive him,
  Than when a mother cries, "You were my only one!"
Lest you may think I prescribe new laws which I have discovered,
  I must disclaim such renown—all my examples are old.
When Agamemnon saw—and what could escape from his vision
  Under whose mighty power lay the dominion of Greece?—
When Agamemnon saw his golden captive, he loved her,
  While her silly old sire stumbled weeping around.
Why do you weep, you hateful old man? Those lovers are happy:
  All your officious zeal, fool, makes it bitter for her.
Calchas, safe in the aid of Achilles, issued the order
  Sending her back to her home, called by her father's demand.
"Well," Agamemnon said, "there is another whose beauty
  Almost is equal to hers, and her name is almost the same.
If Achilles is wise, he will let me have her, and gladly,
  If he is not, let him feel all my imperious power.
As for the rest of you, Greeks, if anyone utters reproaches,
  What is this scepter for, symbol of might in my hand?
For if I am a king, yet have no girl I can sleep with,
  Let Thersites the base sit on the throne in my stead."
So Agamemnon spoke, and took the girl for his solace,
  So his passionate heart welcomed the new for the old.
Learn how to take a new flame from Agamemnon's example,
  While at the fork of the road love goes its separate ways.
Where will you get one, you ask? Go read the books I have written!
  Soon you will find your craft filled to the gunwale with girls.

195

If my counsel is sound, if Apollo's guidance is useful,
 If the words of my mouth have any value for men,
Though you are burnt in a fire that blazes hotter than Etna,
 Try to appear to the girl cold as Siberian ice.
Make her believe you're all right, don't let her know of your anguish;
 Laugh when you want to give way, weeping self-pitiful tears.
I do not give you commands to break off your woes in a moment—
 No such cruel ideas go with my temperate rule.
Try to seem what you are not; pretend the fit has abated,
 So you may really become what you have tried to pretend.
Often, to keep myself from drink, I have feigned to be sleeping;
 Often, while feigning sleep, slumber came over my eyes.
I have laughed at the dupe who made himself think he was loving,
 Watching the fowler fall into the snare he had set.
Love comes into the mind by habit, and habit expels it;
 He who can counterfeit sense comes to his senses in time.
Maybe she tells you to come, and you come on the night she has
  told you,
 Come, and you find the door shut in your face. Never mind!
Don't try to wheedle the door, nor hurl invectives against it,
 Don't lie down there and wait, sleeping all night on the stone.
When the next day comes, assume a cheerful expression,
 Don't let your gesture or words indicate any distress.
She will not be quite so proud if she sees that your interest is
  flagging;
 This is a profit for you, won from my precepts and art.
Still, keep fooling yourself: refuse to concede love is over;
 Often the steed, restrained, fights at the bit and the reins.
Keep your advantage concealed: what you wish, and don't boast
  of, will happen;
 In vain in the sight of the bird is the net of the fowler displayed.
Don't give her any excuse to be smug, and thereby despise you:

Have some pride of your own; make her submit and give in.
Maybe her door is locked? Then saunter carelessly past it.
Has she assigned you a night? Say you're not sure you can
come.
Patience is easy enough, but in case you are lacking that virtue,
Have, in reserve, some girl it takes no patience to win.

How can any one say my lessons are hard to submit to?
Look! I am willing to play even the peacemaker's part.
No two souls are alike, and therefore my arts must be varied;
Thousands the forms of disease, thousands the methods of cure.
Certain bodies, indeed, can hardly be cured by the surgeon;
Potions and herbs alone often bring many relief.
Are you too soft, unable to leave, held fast in your bondage?
Does the cruel boy, Love, stand with his foot on your neck?
Give up the struggle, I say: let the winds have their way with your
canvas;
Where the waves summon you, go; drift with no pull of the
oar.
Satisfy all of your thirst, relieve the fever that burns you.
I have nothing to say—drink from the midst of the stream,
But drink even more than the heart could possibly long for,
Drink till your gullet is full, drink till you slobber your chin.
Keep on enjoying your girl, with nobody there to prevent you,
Let her have all of your nights, let her consume all your days.
Get fed up with it all: excess puts an end to your troubles.
Even though you believe you have had plenty, remain,
Stay, till there's more than enough, till you're perfectly sure you
will never
Ask for it any more; stay till her house is a bore.

Love endures a long time when lack of confidence feeds it:
If you want love to be gone, banish mistrust from your heart.

One who is always afraid of losing out to a rival
  Even Machaon's art hardly is able to cure.
Which of her sons does a mother love more?—the one who is with
    her,
  Or the one in the wars, whence he may never return?
Near the Colline Gate there towers a temple of Venus,
  Hallowed and ancient, a shrine called by a reverent name.
There, in a curious guise, dwells Cupid as healer of heartache,
  There on his torch he pours water cooling the flame.
Thither young men and girls repair when their vows are a burden,
  Seeking forgetfulness there, freed from the hurt in the heart.
He was speaking to me—I doubt if it really was Cupid,
  Hallucination or dream, probably only a dream—
"Ovid, giver of love, Ovid, reliever of lovers.
  Hear what I have to say, add these words to your lore.
Heaven has given to all a certain proportion of trouble;
  Let a man think of his woes, he will be rid of his love.
If he has mortgages due, or creditors hounding for payment,
  Let him devote his mind strictly to thoughts of his debt.
If his father's too strict, or the dower of his wife is too meager,
  Let him keep father or wife well to the front of his mind.
Have you a fruitful estate and vineyards swelling with purple?
  Think of the dangers of drought, think of the damage of frost.
Have you a ship on the sea? The sea is an enemy always;
  Think of the sea and the coast littered with many a wreck.
Fret for a son at the front, or a daughter ready for marriage;
  There are a thousand griefs, worries, distractions, and cares.
What should Paris have done, to acquire a hatred for Helen?
  Thought of his brothers slain, wars and the funeral pyre!"
He had more to say, it seemed, but he faded and vanished,
  Less than the shade of a boy, gone like a ghost from my dream.
What am I going to do? My pilot is lost, and my vessel
  Fares over unknown seas, voyaging perilous ways.

Lonely places are bad, dangerous: shun them, you lovers,
    Leave the deserts alone, you'll be more safe in a crowd.
Better not be alone, for loneliness adds to your passion;
    When there are people about, you will find comfort and aid.
You will be sad, if alone, and the thought of your lady, forsaken,
    Conjure her shade to your sight, summon her ghost to your
      eyes.
Therefore the nights are sad, gloomier far than the daytime
    With no cheerful friends keeping depression away.
Don't run away from good talk, nor shut the door in their faces,
    Don't go and hide in the dark, weeping with pitiful tears.
Always have one good friend, a Pylades for your Orestes;
    This is no trivial boon, using the help of a friend.
What brought Phyllis to doom? The loneliness of the forest.
    That was the cause of her death—she was deserted, alone,
Tossing her hair to the wind, as frenzied as any Bacchante
    At the triennial rites on the Edonian shore.
Now she would look at the sea, the wide expanse of the water,
    Now, in her weariness, lie on the desolate sand.
"Faithless Demophoön!" she would cry to the waves, and their
      deafness
    Could not hear her sobs break the words of her cry.
There was a narrow way, darkened by shade hanging over,
    Where she would often go, sorrowful, down to the sea.
She had walked that way nine times; she cried to her lover,
    Stared at the cord of her gown, stared at the branch of the tree,
Doubted, and shrank from the act, not quite determined, and fear-
      ful,
    Finally, lifted her hands, made them a clasp for her throat.
Poor Sithonian girl! I wish she had not been alone there
    Where the forest leaves mourned for the suicide's doom.
So, be warned by her lot, avoid excessive seclusion,
    Girls who grieve for a man, lovers grieved by a girl.

Once a young patient of mine, obeying my Muse's prescription,
　　Found himself almost cured, almost recovered and well,
Then he had a relapse, met up with some lovers, all eager,
　　Love resuming, once more, arms that were hidden away.
If you don't want to love, don't expose yourself to contagion;
　　Even the beasts of the field often can come to this harm.
Looking at those who are sick, you also may suffer infection;
　　Just from a casual glimpse, frequently, damage is done.
Sometimes to fields that are dry, to clods that are parching and arid
　　Water comes creeping in, sly, from the neighboring stream.
So love creeps in, sly, if you stay at the side of the loved one.
　　We are ingenious folk, cunning to fool ourselves so.
I knew another man who was perfectly cured, but he lingered
　　In the old neighborhood, meeting the lady again.
That was too much for him: ill-healed, the scarified tissue
　　Rankled, a festering wound, one more defeat for my art.
If the house next door is on fire, your own is in danger;
　　You can insure yourself best rapidly running away.
Also, don't go for a walk on the streets she is apt to be strolling,
　　Keep from the set and the round where she is apt to be found.
How does it make any sense to heat yourself up by remembrance?
　　What do you have to do?—Live in a different world.
It is not easy to fast when you sit at an opulent table;
　　It is not easy to thirst, watching the cool of a spring.
Try to hold back a bull when he has a chance at the heifer,
　　Try to hold back a stud hearing the nickering mare!
Nor does it always suffice to reach the shore that you long for,
　　Simply to be on your way, shutting her out of your mind.
No! You must banish the rest, her mother, her nurse, and her sister,
　　Every companion of hers, every close friend that she knew.
Don't let her slave come around, or her maid, with some fanciful
　　　story,
　　Spilling her crocodile tears, saying she misses you so.
Much as you may want to know, don't ever ask what she's doing.

Patience and fortitude! Keep your tongue in your head.
Furthermore, when you state the reasons you had for complaining,
    Make it perfectly clear this is the absolute end.
Cease to complain: you will gain a better vengeance by silence;
    If you indulge in regrets, she will remain in your mind.
Silence is better, too, than saying, "Of course I don't love her!"
    Saying *I don't* too much really implies that *I do.*
Let the fire die out, gradually, little by little,
    Take it easy, don't rush; better be safe, and be slow.
Does not a flash-flood race with wilder rage than a river?
    One is a burst of spate, one a continual flow.
Let love falter and fade, into thin air disappearing;
    Dying by slow degrees, let love falter and fade.
But to hate a girl you once have loved—that is wicked,
    That is the sort of an end fit for a barbarous mind.
It is enough not to care: if your passion is ended in hatred
    Either you're still in love, or you are still a sick man.
Woman and man, once joined in love, should never be hostile—
    That's a disgrace and a shame Venus would never approve.
Often men, filing complaints, are still in love with their women;
    When no quarrel comes in, love slips forgotten away.
I can remember a case: a lady was borne in her litter
    When my client approached, bearing a summons in hand,
Uttering terrible threats, "You bitch, get out of that litter!"
    She stepped down, and at once he had nothing to say,
Dropped his hands at his sides, and dropped the writ of injunction,
    Took her at once in his arms, murmuring, "Darling, you win."
It is safer, more fit, to break off without any contention;
    Don't, from the chambers of love, rush to the courts of the law.
Let her keep the gifts you have given, don't argue about them;
    Such a diminutive loss proves a magnificent gain.
And if you meet later on, if some accident brings you together,
    Try to remember and use all my instruction in arms.
Now you have need of arms: fight on, O bravest of heroes,

Be an Achilles and strike, Penthesilea will fall.
Think of your rival now, think of that obdurate threshold,
  Think of your foolish prayers, calling the gods to your aid,
Don't arrange your hair on the chance that perhaps you will meet
      her,
  Don't let the drape of your gown call for attention or talk,
Take no trouble at all to please the girl—she's a stranger,
  Nothing in your young life, only one of the herd.

What is the greatest block that stands in the way of our efforts?
  Let me bring home to you what your own history shows.
We are slow to break off, because we hope that they love us,
  Each of us fond of himself—oh, what a credulous crew!
Don't believe their words (for what could be more deceitful?),
  Don't believe their vows, oaths that they swear to the gods,
Don't be taken in by the tears of these lachrymose creatures,
  Women can teach their eyes how to redden and weep.
They have a thousand arts for besieging the minds of their lovers,
  They are the waves that wear down even inveterate stone.
Give no reasons at all to explain your decision to leave her,
  Voice no grievance, but keep grievance alive in your heart,
Make no itemized list of her faults, for fear she correct them;
  First thing you know, you will be pleading her virtues again.
He who is silent is strong, but the lover who utters reproaches
  Seems to weaken his case, almost determined to lose.
No Ulysses I, to steal his arrows from Cupid,
  I would not clip his wings, I would not loosen his bow,
I would not douse his torch, quenching its flame in the river,
  Still, what I sing is good sense; listen to me as I sing.
And, O health-giving god, Apollo, be present to help me!
  Let the quiver and lyre come to the aid of my song,
Just as they always have done; I know the signs of the godhead,
  Hearing the quiver and lyre, I know that Apollo is here.
If you compare the wool dyed dark in the vats of Amyclae

With the purple from Tyre, see its inferior hue!
So, compare your girl with the ones who really are beauties—
    It will be only a while till you regard her with shame.
Juno, Minerva—they both might have seemed attractive to Paris;
    Neither, when Venus was there, offered the slightest appeal.
Don't compare looks alone, but also character, talent,
    Only, don't let your love bias the verdict you give.
Next comes a trivial point, but perhaps it may serve your advantage:
    Others have told me as much; it helped to cure me, I know.
Don't read over again those fondly cherished old letters;
    Letters read over again move the most obdurate minds.
Put them all in the fire, however reluctant your spirit,
    Say, as you put them there, "This is the pyre of my love."
Althea burned the brand that ensured the life of her offspring;
    Are you a coward, to fear burning some treacherous words?
If you can do it, remove, as well, her portrait, or likeness;
    Why let an image, mute, rouse the regret in your heart?
Places that say no word can hurt you; better avoid them,
    Give them no chance to suggest days that are over and gone,
Telling you, "Here she lay; we slept in that bedroom together,
    That was the place where, at night, she gave me boundless de-
        light."
Love is renewed afresh, and the wounds made worse, by remem-
    brance;
    If you are weak you can be hurt by the slightest mistake.
Just as an ember, all gray, will crimson under the sulphur,
    Springing to life again, flaming to ardor and fire,
So, unless you avoid whatever rekindles your passion,
    Flames which were all but out presently flare up again.
Where the false fires burn, the danger of shipwreck is greatest,
    Mariners also fear seas that are only too calm:
Look on pleasures past as the Clashing Rocks, or the waters
    Where, each side of the strait, Scylla, Charybdis await.

There are some things no man can bring about by an order,
    Yet, if they happen by chance, they can be profit and gain.
Phaedra, bereft of her wealth, would have had no desire for her
        stepson;
    Riches supply the fare feeding the wantonest love.
Why did no man take Hecale, and no woman Iras?
    That is no puzzle at all; one was a beggar, one poor.
Poverty has no store to replenish the passion of lovers—
    Still, it is hardly worth while taking that treatment to cure.
But it is worth while to avoid the stage and the playhouse
    Till you are sure your heart holds not a remnant of love.
Zithers and flutes and lyres will weaken the hardiest nature,
    So will voices and limbs moved to the cadence of song.
Lovers are always portrayed in the lively movements of dancing,
    Where the actor's art shows the temptations, the risk.
This I hate to say, but have nothing to do with the poets!
    I am willing to ban even the works of my pen.
Run from them all; don't trust Callimachus, lackey of Cupid,
    Or that fellow from Cos; he is as bad, if not worse.
Sappho, in my own case, helped me win over one woman,
    Nor was Anacreon's song ever a celibate strain.
Who could be safe if he read the tender verse of Tibullus?
    Who could read Gallus unmoved? What about work of my
        own?
If our patron, Apollo, has not deluded his poet,
    One of our principal griefs comes from our rivals in love.
But you must not let yourself imagine a rival,
    Better believe she lies all by herself in her bed.
When Hermione left to become the bride of another,
    Then Orestes' love burst into passionate flame.
Menelaus could sail, alone, to Crete without Helen;
    Why should he grieve over that? He could be absent for long.
When Paris carried her off, that was a different story.

Through another man's love he learned the depth of his own.
There was a bitter lament from Achilles when Briseis, taken,
     Brought Agamemnon's bed pleasure he had to forego.
He had good reason to grieve, believe me; King Agamemnon
     Did what any man would, barring a eunuch or queer.
Certainly I would have done it, and I am no wiser than he was.
     That, more than anything else, furthered the feud and the
          grudge,
For, in sending her back, he swore that he never had touched her,
     Swore by his scepter—why not? Who calls a scepter a god?
May the gods grant you the power to pass by her threshold, un-
          heeding,
     Keep your determined stride firm on the course you have set.
Why, of course you can do it! You only have to be willing,
     Willing, determined, and brave, setting the spur to your steed.
Fancy in one of those caves the Lotus-eaters are hiding,
     Fancy that Sirens are there—help out your sail with the oar.
If in the past you grieved because you were hurt by a rival,
     I would implore you now, cease to regard him as foe,
Give him hail-fellow-well-met, in spite of your lingering hatred;
     When you can give him a kiss, then you are perfectly well!

Then there's the matter of food, and I, as befits a physician,
     Tell you what you should avoid, what you may safely consume.
Onions, the native kind and the foreign, are equally harmful;
     Rocket is apt to inflame; shun aphrodisiacs, too.
Rue you can safely take—it helps to sharpen the eyesight;
     Anaphrodisiacs, too, lulling the passions to rest.
What about Bacchus' gift, you ask? My answer is ready;
     Sooner than you may expect, we shall have finished our task.
Wine prepares the heart for love, if you don't overdo it,
     If your spirits are not deadened and buried in wine.
Fire can be fanned by a wind, as fire, by a wind, is extinguished,

A gentler breeze fans the flame, a heavier puts it to death.
Either get thoroughly drunk, or be a teetotal abstainer:
  Anything in between causes the passions to rise.

So, I have finished my work: hang wreaths on the prow of my ves-
    sel;
  We have come to the port whither my voyage was bound.
Soon you will pay your vows, as duty requires, to your poet,
  Women and men alike, healed by the power of my song.

MIDLAND BOOKS